BRITISH HISTORICAL PORTRAITS

BRITISH
HISTORICAL PORTRAITS

A SELECTION FROM THE
NATIONAL PORTRAIT GALLERY
WITH BIOGRAPHICAL NOTES

CAMBRIDGE

PUBLISHED FOR THE NATIONAL PORTRAIT GALLERY
AT THE UNIVERSITY PRESS
1957

PUBLISHED BY

THE SYNDICS OF THE CAMBRIDGE UNIVERSITY PRESS

Bentley House, 200 Euston Road, London, N.W. 1
American Branch: 32 East 57th Street, New York 22, N.Y.

Printed in Great Britain at the University Press, Cambridge
(Brooke Crutchley, University Printer)

FOREWORD

It is a hundred years since it was resolved, on the initiative of the 5th Earl Stanhope, to form 'a Gallery of the Portraits of the most eminent Persons in British History.'

The collection now numbers some four thousand portraits, affording incidentally an epitome of the history of the art of portraiture in England from its inception to the present time. Famous men and women of all professions and pursuits are represented, in accordance with the precepts of Thomas Carlyle, by 'a good portrait if such exists; failing that, even an indifferent if sincere one'. Inevitably a few great names are missing since there are those of whom no authentic portrait from life is known, and others whose portraits are elsewhere.

About one tenth of the portraits in the Gallery are reproduced here, arranged in approximately chronological order: following the plates, and in the same order, are notes in which each sitter's historical significance is briefly indicated.

March 1956

THE PORTRAITS

1   KING HENRY IV

2   KING HENRY V

3   KING HENRY VI

4   KING EDWARD IV

9

5   KING RICHARD III

6   LADY MARGARET BEAUFORT

7   KING HENRY VII

8   KING HENRY VIII

9   ANNE BOLEYN   10   CATHERINE OF ARAGON

11   THOMAS CROMWELL,   12   THOMAS WOLSEY
EARL OF ESSEX

11

13   SIR THOMAS MORE WITH HIS FAMILY AND DESCENDANTS

14   REGINALD POLE

15   KING EDWARD VI

16 QUEEN MARY I

17 THOMAS CRANMER

18   QUEEN ELIZABETH I

14

19 MARY, QUEEN OF SCOTS

20 THOMAS HOWARD,
DUKE OF NORFOLK

21 SIR FRANCIS WALSINGHAM

22   WILLIAM CECIL, LORD
      BURGHLEY

23   SIR THOMAS GRESHAM

24 ROBERT CECIL, EARL OF
SALISBURY

25 SIR RICHARD GRENVILLE

26   SIR PHILIP SIDNEY

27   ROBERT DUDLEY, EARL OF
     LEICESTER

28   SIR FRANCIS DRAKE

29   ROBERT DEVEREUX, EARL OF ESSEX   30   SIR WALTER RALEIGH

To the Reader.

This Figure, that thou here seest put,
 It was for gentle Shakespeare cut;
Wherein the Grauer had a strife
 with Nature, to out-doo the life:
O, could he but haue drawne his wit
 As well in brasse, as he hath hit
Hisface ; the Print would then surpasse
 All, that was euer writ in brasse.
But, since he cannot, Reader, looke
 Not on his Picture, but his Booke.

B. I.

31   WILLIAM SHAKESPEARE

32 BENJAMIN JONSON   33 JOHN DONNE

34 INIGO JONES   35 MICHAEL DRAYTON

21

2-2

36   KING JAMES I

37 THE SOMERSET HOUSE CONFERENCE

38 ANNE OF DENMARK   39 ELIZABETH, QUEEN OF BOHEMIA

40   FRANCIS BACON, VISCOUNT ST ALBAN

41   GEORGE VILLIERS, IST DUKE OF BUCKINGHAM

42   HENRIETTA MARIA

26

43   KING CHARLES I

27

44 THOMAS WENTWORTH,
EARL OF STRAFFORD

45 WILLIAM LAUD

28

46   OLIVER CROMWELL

47   THOMAS HOWARD,
EARL OF ARUNDEL

48   SIR ANTHONY VANDYCK

49   JOHN MILTON

50   THOMAS, LORD FAIRFAX
OF CAMERON

51   JOHN EVELYN

52   SIR THOMAS BROWNE AND HIS WIFE

53   THOMAS HOBBES

54   WILLIAM HARVEY

31

55   SAMUEL BUTLER

56   IZAAK WALTON

57   JOHN BUNYAN

58   SIR PETER LELY

59   PRINCE RUPERT

60   KING CHARLES II

61   CATHERINE OF
BRAGANZA

62   NELL GWYN

63   LOUISE DE KEROUALLE,
     DUCHESS OF
     PORTSMOUTH

64 GEORGE MONCK, DUKE OF ALBEMARLE

65 EDWARD HYDE, EARL
OF CLARENDON

66 HENRIETTA, DUCHESS
OF ORLEANS

67   JOHN MAITLAND, DUKE OF
LAUDERDALE

68   ANTHONY ASHLEY-
COOPER, EARL OF
SHAFTESBURY

69   SIR WILLIAM TEMPLE   70   SAMUEL PEPYS

71   ANNA MARIA TALBOT, COUNTESS   72   GEORGE VILLIERS, 2ND DUKE
OF SHREWSBURY   OF BUCKINGHAM

38

73   KING JAMES II

74   ANNE, DUCHESS OF YORK

75   MARY OF MODENA

40

76 GEORGE, LORD JEFFREYS

77 JAMES SCOTT, DUKE OF
MONMOUTH

78   JOHN DRYDEN

79   JOHN LOCKE   80   HENRY PURCELL

42

81   SIR CHRISTOPHER WREN

82   SIR ISAAC NEWTON   83   SIR GODFREY KNELLER

43

84   KING WILLIAM III

85   QUEEN MARY II

86   WILLIAM BENTINCK,
     EARL OF PORTLAND

87   CHARLES MONTAGU,
     EARL OF HALIFAX

88 QUEEN ANNE AND
WILLIAM, DUKE OF
GLOUCESTER

89 PRINCE GEORGE OF
DENMARK

90 JOHN CHURCHILL, DUKE
OF MARLBOROUGH

91 SARAH, DUCHESS OF
MARLBOROUGH

92   JAMES, EARL STANHOPE

93   SIR GEORGE ROOKE

94   WILLIAM DAMPIER

95   HENRY ST JOHN, VISCOUNT
BOLINGBROKE

96   ROBERT HARLEY, EARL OF
OXFORD

97   JACOB TONSON

98   SIR JOHN VANBRUGH

99   JOSEPH ADDISON

100   SIR RICHARD STEELE

101   JONATHAN SWIFT

102   WILLIAM CONGREVE

103   DANIEL DEFOE

104 MATTHEW PRIOR

105 MICHAEL DAHL

106   KING GEORGE I

107   PRINCE JAMES FRANCIS EDWARD STUART AND HIS SISTER

108 JONATHAN RICHARDSON

109 GEORGE VERTUE

110 COLLEY CIBBER

111 ALEXANDER POPE

112   SIR HANS SLOANE

113   GEORGE BERKELEY

114 GEORGE FREDERICK HANDEL

115 ISAAC WATTS

116 JAMES GIBBS

117 KING GEORGE II

118   CAROLINE OF ANSPACH

119 AUGUSTA, PRINCESS OF
WALES

120 FREDERICK LEWIS,
PRINCE OF WALES

121   PRINCE CHARLES EDWARD STUART   122   GEORGE WADE

123   DUNCAN FORBES   124   WILLIAM AUGUSTUS, DUKE OF
                                    CUMBERLAND

125 ROBERT WALPOLE, EARL
OF ORFORD

126 JOHN CARTERET, EARL
GRANVILLE

127   GEORGE, LORD ANSON

128   EDWARD VERNON

129   ROBERT, LORD CLIVE

130   JEFFREY, LORD AMHERST   131   STRINGER LAWRENCE

132   WILLIAM PULTENEY, EARL OF BATH

133   RICHARD TEMPLE, VISCOUNT COBHAM

134   PHILIP DORMER STANHOPE,
EARL OF CHESTERFIELD

135   WILLIAM PITT, EARL OF CHATHAM

136   THOMAS PELHAM-HOLLES,
DUKE OF NEWCASTLE

137   JAMES WOLFE

138   PEG WOFFINGTON

139   TOBIAS GEORGE SMOLLETT

140   KITTY FISHER

141   WILLIAM HOGARTH

142   SAMUEL RICHARDSON

143 GEORGE WHITEFIELD

144 JOHN WESLEY

145 CHARLOTTE OF
MECKLENBURG-STRELITZ

146 KING GEORGE III

147 JOHN GLYNN, JOHN WILKES AND JOHN HORNE TOOKE

148 FREDERICK NORTH, EARL OF GUILFORD

149   SIR JOHN FIELDING

150   SIR WILLIAM
BLACKSTONE

151   WARREN HASTINGS

152   EDMUND BURKE

153   CHARLES WATSON-WENTWORTH,
MARQUESS OF ROCKINGHAM

74

154   WILLIAM PITT

155   CHARLES JAMES FOX

156   ARTHUR PHILLIP

157   JAMES COOK

158   ADAM, VISCOUNT DUNCAN

159 RICHARD, EARL HOWE

160 HORATIO, VISCOUNT NELSON

161   EMMA, LADY HAMILTON

162   BENJAMIN FRANKLIN

163   GEORGE WASHINGTON

164 SIR WILLIAM HAMILTON

165   JOSEPH PRIESTLEY

166   SIR WILLIAM HERSCHEL

167   JOHN SMEATON

168   SIR RICHARD ARKWRIGHT

169   JOHN HUNTER

170   JAMES WATT

171   JOHN HOWARD

172   THOMAS CLARKSON

173   THOMAS GRAY

174   HORACE WALPOLE,
EARL OF ORFORD

175   ROBERT RAIKES

176   ADAM SMITH

177   JOSIAH WEDGWOOD

178   EDWARD GIBBON

179   ROBERT BURNS

180　WILLIAM COWPER

181　LAURENCE STERNE

182   ROBERT ADAM

183   RICHARD WILSON   184   THOMAS GAINSBOROUGH

185   SIR JOSHUA REYNOLDS

186   DR SAMUEL JOHNSON

187 CHARLES BURNEY

188 FANNY BURNEY

189 OLIVER GOLDSMITH

190 JAMES BOSWELL

191   JOSEPH WRIGHT

192   JOHN ZOFFANY

193   JOHN OPIE

194   JAMES NORTHCOTE

195   GEORGE ROMNEY

196   NATHANIEL HONE

197   ALLAN RAMSAY

198   DAVID GARRICK

199   JOHN PHILIP KEMBLE

200   RICHARD BRINSLEY SHERIDAN

201   THOMAS AUGUSTINE ARNE

202   PERDITA ROBINSON

203   SARAH SIDDONS   204   ELIZABETH FARREN

205   FREDERIC, DUKE OF YORK

206   ERNEST AUGUSTUS, DUKE OF
CUMBERLAND

207   KING GEORGE IV

208 PRINCESS CHARLOTTE OF
WALES

209 CAROLINE OF BRUNSWICK

210   ARTHUR WELLESLEY, DUKE OF WELLINGTON

211   SIR JOHN MOORE   212   SIR GRAHAM MOORE

213   GEORGE CANNING

214   ROBERT BANKS JENKINSON,
      EARL OF LIVERPOOL

215   ROBERT STEWART, MARQUESS
      OF LONDONDERRY

216   WILLIAM HUSKISSON

217 SIR THOMAS STAMFORD
      BINGLEY RAFFLES

218 JEREMY BENTHAM

219   WILLIAM WILBERFORCE

220   WILLIAM BLAKE   221   MARY GODWIN

222 WILLIAM WORDSWORTH

223 CHARLES LAMB

224 SAMUEL TAYLOR COLERIDGE

225 ROBERT SOUTHEY

226 SIR WALTER SCOTT   227 GEORGE GORDON, LORD BYRON

228 JOHN KEATS   229 PERCY BYSSHE SHELLEY

230   JOHN SELL COTMAN

231   JOHN CROME

232   JOHN CONSTABLE

233   WILLIAM HAZLITT

234 JOHN NASH

235 JANE AUSTEN   236 JOSEPH MALLORD WILLIAM TURNER

101   7·2

237   KING WILLIAM IV

238   ADELAIDE OF SAXE-MEININGEN

239   MARIA LOUISA VICTORIA,
DUCHESS OF KENT

240   EDWARD, DUKE OF KENT

241   QUEEN VICTORIA

242   PRINCE ALBERT OF SAXE-COBURG-GOTHA

105

243   WILLIAM LAMB, VISCOUNT MELBOURNE

244   CHARLES, EARL GREY

245   JOHN GEORGE LAMBTON,
EARL OF DURHAM

246   THOMAS ARNOLD

247   SIR ROBERT PEEL

248   HENRY JOHN TEMPLE,
VISCOUNT PALMERSTON

249   SYDNEY SMITH

250   ELIZABETH FRY

251   SIR JOHN FRANKLIN

252   MICHAEL FARADAY

253   SIR HUMPHRY DAVY

254   GEORGE STEPHENSON

255   JOHN KEBLE   256   EDWARD BOUVERIE PUSEY

257   ROBERT OWEN   258   JOHN RUSKIN

259 THOMAS CARLYLE

260 JOHN STUART MILL

261 THOMAS BABINGTON,
LORD MACAULAY

262   'GEORGE ELIOT'

263   ELIZABETH CLEGHORN GASKELL

264   CHARLOTTE MARY YONGE

265   EDWARD BULWER-LYTTON,
LORD LYTTON

266   DANTE GABRIEL ROSSETTI   267   CHRISTINA GEORGINA ROSSETTI
AND HER MOTHER

268   ROBERT BROWNING   269   ELIZABETH BARRETT BROWNING

270   THE BRONTË SISTERS

271   WILLIAM MAKEPEACE THACKERAY

272   ANTHONY TROLLOPE

273   CHARLES DICKENS

274   ALFRED, LORD TENNYSON   275   ALGERNON CHARLES SWINBURNE

276   WILLIAM EWART GLADSTONE

277   BENJAMIN DISRAELI, EARL
        OF BEACONSFIELD

278   RICHARD COBDEN

279   JOHN BRIGHT

280   ROBERT GASCOYNE-CECIL,
MARQUESS OF SALISBURY

281   JOHN LAIRD MAIR,
LORD LAWRENCE

282   CHARLES GEORGE GORDON

283   SIR RICHARD FRANCIS BURTON

284   DAVID LIVINGSTONE

285   CECIL JOHN RHODES

286   CHARLES ROBERT DARWIN

287   THOMAS HENRY HUXLEY

288   JOSEPH, LORD LISTER   289   FLORENCE NIGHTINGALE

290   WILLIAM THOMSON, LORD KELVIN

291   JOHN FREDERICK DENISON MAURICE

292   ANTHONY ASHLEY-COOPER,
EARL OF SHAFTESBURY

293   WILLIAM BOOTH

294   JOHN HENRY NEWMAN

295   EDWARD HENRY MANNING

296   CHARLES KINGSLEY

297   CHARLES READE

298 WILLIAM HOLMAN–HUNT

299 SIR EDWIN HENRY LANDSEER

300   SIR EDWARD COLEY BURNE-JONES

301   SIR JOHN EVERETT MILLAIS

302   SIR CHARLES HALLÉ

303 MRS BEETON

304 JENNY LIND

305   SIR WILLIAM SCHWENK GILBERT

306   SIR ARTHUR SEYMOUR SULLIVAN

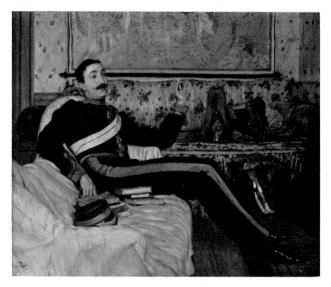

307   FREDERICK GUSTAVUS BURNABY

308   WILLIAM GILBERT GRACE

309 FREDERIC, LORD LEIGHTON

310 GEORGE FREDERIC WATTS

311 WILLIAM MORRIS

312   MATTHEW ARNOLD

313   SAMUEL BUTLER

314   WILLIAM HENRY HUDSON

315   SIR HENRY RIDER HAGGARD

316   ROBERT LOUIS BALFOUR STEVENSON

317   GEORGE MEREDITH

318   THOMAS HARDY

319   MRS HUMPHREY WARD

320   JOSEPH RUDYARD
KIPLING

321　OSCAR WILDE

322　'LEWIS CARROLL'

323　SIR JOHN TENNIEL

324   JAMES ABBOTT MCNEILL WHISTLER

325   EDWARD LEAR

326   PHIL MAY

327   SIR HENRY IRVING

328   NELLIE FARREN

329   DAME ELLEN ALICE TERRY

330 DINAH MARIA MULOCK

331 OCTAVIA HILL

332 JOSEPHINE ELIZABETH BUTLER

137

333   HORATIO HERBERT,
       EARL KITCHENER

334   FREDERICK SLEIGH,
       EARL ROBERTS

335   JOSEPH CHAMBERLAIN

336   JOHN BURNS

337   KING EDWARD VII

338 ALEXANDRA OF
DENMARK

339 GEORGE NATHANIEL,
MARQUESS CURZON

340 ROBERT FALCON SCOTT

341 SIR JOHN WILLIAM ALCOCK

342   DOUGLAS, EARL HAIG

343   DAVID, EARL BEATTY

344   JOHN FRENCH, EARL OF YPRES

345   EDMUND HENRY HYNMAN,
VISCOUNT ALLENBY

346   COVENTRY PATMORE

347   SIR ARTHUR WING PINERO

348   HENRY JAMES

349   WILLIAM WYMARK JACOBS

350   THE SELECTING JURY OF THE NEW ENGLISH ART CLUB

351   WALTER RICHARD SICKERT   352   PHILIP WILSON STEER

353   THE ROYAL FAMILY AT BUCKINGHAM PALACE

King George V, Queen Mary, the Duke of Windsor (Edward VIII)
and the Princess Royal

146

354 GILBERT KEITH CHESTERTON, THE HON. MAURICE BARING AND
JOSEPH HILAIRE PIERRE BELLOC

355 RUPERT BROOKE

356 GEORGE BERNARD SHAW   357 ALFRED EDWARD HOUSMAN

358   JOSEPH CONRAD   359   ENOCH ARNOLD BENNETT

360   SIR JAMES MATTHEW BARRIE   361   THOMAS EDWARD LAWRENCE

362   DAVID, EARL LLOYD GEORGE

363   HERBERT HENRY ASQUITH,
EARL OF OXFORD

364   EDWARD, VISCOUNT GREY

365   RICHARD BURDON, VISCOUNT
HALDANE

366 JAMES RAMSAY MACDONALD

367 JOHN BUCHAN, LORD
TWEEDSMUIR

368 STANLEY, EARL BALDWIN

369 GEORGE LANSBURY

370   SIR WILLIAM HENRY BRAGG

371   SIR JOSEPH JOHN THOMSON

372   ERNEST, LORD RUTHERFORD

373   SIR RONALD ROSS

374   BEATRIX POTTER

375   DAME ETHEL MARY SMYTH

376   EMMELINE PANKHURST

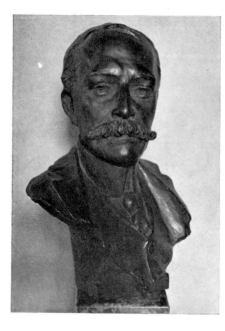

377   SIR EDWARD WILLIAM ELGAR

378   SIR HENRY JOSEPH WOOD

379   ADELINE VIRGINIA WOOLF   380   WILLIAM BUTLER YEATS

381   JAMES JOYCE

382   CONVERSATION PIECE AT THE ROYAL LODGE, WINDSOR

King George VI, Queen Elizabeth the Queen Mother, Her Majesty
Queen Elizabeth II, and Princess Margaret

BIOGRAPHICAL NOTES

KING HENRY IV. 1367–1413.

Son and heir of John of Gaunt, Duke of Lancaster and grandson of Edward III. Upon his father's death in 1399 he landed in England from exile abroad, forced Richard II to abdicate and was crowned first Lancastrian King. His reign was one of perpetual conflict. He founded the Order of the Bath and was patron of Chaucer and John Gower.

PLATE 1. *Painting by an unknown artist.* $22\frac{1}{2} \times 17\frac{1}{2}$ in. No. 310.

KING HENRY V. 1387–1422.

Eldest son of Henry IV. He embarked to conquer France and won the battle of Agincourt in 1415. In 1420 he married Katherine of Valois, daughter of King Charles VI, who accepted him as heir to the throne of France to the exclusion of the Dauphin. At home he repressed the Lollards, reorganised the English navy and was patron of poets.

PLATE 2. *Painting by an unknown artist.* 22×16 in. No. 545.

KING HENRY VI. 1421–1471.

When one year old he succeeded his father, Henry V. All his French possessions except Calais were lost by 1453. In 1449 Richard, 3rd Duke of York, claimed the English throne, and in 1455 defeated Henry at St Albans, the first battle of the Wars of the Roses. Richard's son, Edward IV, was proclaimed King in 1461, and Henry became a fugitive. In 1471 his only son was killed at Tewkesbury, and he himself was murdered. He founded Eton in 1440 and King's College, Cambridge, in 1441.

PLATE 3. *Painting by an unknown artist.* $12\frac{3}{4} \times 10$ in. No. 2457.

KING EDWARD IV. 1442–1483.

Son of Richard, 3rd Duke of York, on whose death in 1460 he took command of the Yorkists. Victories at Mortimer Cross and Towton in 1461 won him the throne which he held securely only after his victories at Barnet and Tewkesbury and the murder of Henry VI in 1471. He kept his realm in order, encouraged trade and amassed a fortune.

PLATE 4. *Painting by an unknown artist.* $12\frac{1}{2} \times 10$ in. No. 3542.

KING RICHARD III. 1452–1485.

Duke of Gloucester: youngest brother of Edward IV, on whose death he became Protector. He lodged his nephews, the young King Edward V and the Duke of York, in the Tower: the mystery surrounding their murder remains unsolved, despite the wealth of ingenious speculation and impassioned special-pleading, on both sides, which has accumulated down the ages. He was crowned in 1483 and revealed good qualities during an uneasy reign of only two years. He was defeated and slain at Bosworth, the last battle of the Wars of the Roses.

PLATE 5. *Painting by an unknown artist.* 25 × 18 in. No. 148.

LADY MARGARET BEAUFORT. 1443–1509.

Heiress of John of Gaunt: in 1455 she married Edmund Tudor, Earl of Richmond: their son, Henry VII, was the first Tudor monarch. Active in politics, she was also patroness of learning, as witness the Lady Margaret foundations and Christ's and St John's Colleges, Cambridge.

PLATE 6. *Painting by an unknown artist.* $26\frac{1}{2} \times 21\frac{3}{4}$ in. No. 551.

KING HENRY VII. 1457?–1509.

Son of Edmund Tudor and Margaret Beaufort, and from 1471 head of the house of Lancaster. For some years a refugee in Brittany, he invaded England in 1485, defeated Richard III at Bosworth, and was crowned King. His marriage in 1486 with Elizabeth of York, Edward IV's daughter, united the Houses of York and Lancaster. The treaties and matrimonial alliances he effected promoted trade and peace. He was patron of learning and added his chapel to Westminster Abbey.

PLATE 7. *Painting by Michiel Sitium, 1505.* $14\frac{1}{2} \times 9\frac{1}{2}$ in. No. 416.

KING HENRY VIII. 1491–1547.

Second son of Henry VII, whom he succeeded. No son by his first wife, Catherine of Aragon, survived infancy and he determined to have the marriage annulled. This involved the break with Rome and his claim to supreme headship of the English Church, the execution of More and Fisher and the dissolution of the monasteries. His talent and early prowess are famous: his six marriages and the savagery of his late years notorious. He was a musician and dialectic author and he completed Christ College, Oxford.

PLATE 8. *Painting after Holbein.* $10\frac{3}{4} \times 7\frac{1}{2}$ in. No. 157.

ANNE BOLEYN. 1507–1536.

Second Queen of Henry VIII and mother of Queen Elizabeth I. She was the King's mistress for some years before she was married to him by Archbishop Cranmer in 1533. She had no son; three years after the marriage she was charged with infidelity and beheaded.

PLATE 9. *Painting by an unknown artist.* 21 × 16 in. No. 668.

CATHERINE OF ARAGON. 1485–1536.

Daughter of Ferdinand and Isabella of Spain. In 1501 she was married to Arthur, Prince of Wales, who died the following year; in 1509 she became the first wife of Henry VIII by whom she was the mother of Mary I. In 1526 Henry, desiring a male heir, determined to divorce her. Rome refusing sanction, the matter was made one for Canterbury, and in 1533 Cranmer complied.

PLATE 10. *Painting by an unknown artist.* 22¼ × 17¼ in. No. 163.

THOMAS CROMWELL, EARL OF ESSEX. 1485?–1540.

He rose to power in Wolsey's service—found a way out of his wreck to rise in—and became the ruthless servant of a ruthless monarch. Besides effecting the dissolution of the monasteries, he engineered Henry VIII's divorce of Catherine of Aragon, the fall of Anne Boleyn and the unfortunate marriage with Anne of Cleeves which led to his own downfall and execution. He revolutionised the method of government, replacing the outmoded machinery of the medieval household by an efficient bureaucracy.

PLATE 11. *Painting after Holbein.* 29½ × 23 in. No. 1727.

THOMAS WOLSEY. 1475?–1530.

Statesman and Archbishop of York. From chaplain to Henry VII he mounted to the rank of cardinal and Lord Chancellor. He was Henry VIII's chief minister till his failure over the divorce of Queen Catherine turned the King against him. He died on his way to answer a trumped-up charge of treason. He partly built Hampton Court and began Christ Church, Oxford.

PLATE 12. *Painting by an unknown artist.* 32½ × 21¾ in. No. 32.

SIR THOMAS MORE. 1478–1535

Scholar and statesman, friend of Erasmus and Holbein, and the author of *Utopia*. In 1518 a Privy Councillor, he became the intimate friend of Henry VIII, and was Lord Chancellor from 1529 till 1532. Fatally entangled in the questions of Queen Catherine's divorce, the Papal supremacy and the succession through Anne Boleyn, he was found guilty of treason and executed. He was Canonised in 1935.

PLATE 13. *Painting by an unknown artist, 1593, part after Holbein.* 89½ × 131½ in. No. 2765.

REGINALD POLE. 1500–1558.

Opposed to Henry's VIII's divorce, and consequent Church policy, he stayed abroad till Mary's succession. He was made cardinal in 1536 and was Papal Legate to the Low Countries in 1536–7. In 1549 he was all but elected Pope; in 1556 he became Archbishop of Canterbury. His great aim was to reconcile the Church of England with Rome.

PLATE 14. *Painting by an unknown artist.* 18 × 14½ in. No. 220.

KING EDWARD VI. 1537–1553.

Son of Henry VIII by his third wife, Jane Seymour. He was ten years old when he came to the throne and during his brief reign England was ruled in turn by Protector Somerset (beheaded in 1552) and Dudley, Duke of Northumberland, on whose direction Edward devised the crown to Lady Jane Grey. He was a promising scholar and a musician; the English Book of Common Prayer was first published in his reign.

PLATE 15. *Painting after Holbein.* 18 × 13 in. No. 442.

QUEEN MARY I. 1516–1558.

Daughter of Henry VIII by his first wife, Catherine of Aragon. Edward VI had devised the crown to Lady Jane Grey, but the country revolted and Mary was proclaimed Queen in accordance with an act of 1544. She married her Spanish cousin, Philip II, as fanatical a Catholic as she, and, bent on uprooting Protestantism, sanctioned the hideous persecutions that made her name terrible. She died childless.

PLATE 16. *Painting by an unknown artist, 1544.* 27 × 21 in. No. 428.

THOMAS CRANMER. 1489–1556.

Serving Henry VIII's interests as regards the supremacy of the English Church, his divorce and other matrimonial ventures, Cranmer was made Archbishop of Canterbury in 1533. After the death of Edward VI he agreed to the attempt to exclude Princess Mary from the succession in favour of Lady Jane Grey. For this and for his heresies he was degraded, whereupon he recanted, but in vain, and he died at the stake repudiating his recantation. The Edwardian Prayer Books show him to be one of our finest prose writers.

PLATE 17. *Painting by Gerlach Flicke, 1546.* $38\frac{1}{2} \times 29\frac{1}{2}$ in. No. 535.

QUEEN ELIZABETH I. 1533–1603.

Daughter of Henry VIII by his second wife, Anne Boleyn. From childhood she learned to endure a world of intrigue and mortal danger. Coming to the throne in 1558 at a most critical hour in England's history, she restored Protestantism and turned her skill to uniting her people, making her country solvent and balking foreign interference. She and her ministers and sea captains did much towards making England a great European power.

PLATE 18. *Painting by an unknown artist, c. 1593.* 93×59 in. No. 2561.

MARY, QUEEN OF SCOTS. 1542–1587.

Daughter of James V of Scotland and Mary of Guise. She succeeded her father at a week old; at six years she was taken to France and at sixteen was married to the Dauphin (later François II, d. 1560); after the death of Mary I she styled herself Queen of England. She was back in Scotland in 1561, intent on restoring Catholicism. In 1565 she married Henry Stuart, Lord Darnley, and their son became James VI and I. After the murder of Darnley in 1567 she married the Earl of Bothwell. Forced to abdicate, she fled to England in 1568 and was perpetually imprisoned. For nearly twenty years she was the hub of plots against Elizabeth who finally consented to her execution.

PLATE 19. *Painting attributed to P. Oudry, 1578.* $36\frac{1}{2} \times 35$ in. No. 429.

THOMAS HOWARD, 4TH DUKE OF NORFOLK. 1536–1572.

A cousin of Queen Elizabeth I (through her mother) and the sole surviving duke in her reign. He plotted with Philip of Spain and the Catholic party, and schemed to marry Mary, Queen of Scots. The conspiracy was crushed, but the part he played later in Ridolfi's plot led to his execution.

PLATE 20. *Painting by an unknown artist.* $21 \times 16\frac{3}{4}$ in. No. 1732.

SIR FRANCIS WALSINGHAM. 1530?–1590.

At first in Burghley's foreign intelligence service, he became a Secretary of State and as head of a most efficient secret service exposed

Ridolfi's conspiracy, 1569, and unearthed the Babington plot, 1586, thereby securing the execution of Mary, Queen of Scots. In opposition to Burghley on the Privy Council, he favoured overt war with Spain.

PLATE 21. *Painting by an unknown artist.* $29\frac{1}{2} \times 24\frac{1}{2}$ in. No. 1807.

WILLIAM CECIL, 1st BARON BURGHLEY. 1520–1598.

In 1548 he became secretary to Protector Somerset. He was Secretary of State under Edward VI and Queen Elizabeth and from 1572 Lord High Treasurer till his death. He was Queen Elizabeth's servant and adviser for forty years; no other Prince, she said, had such a counsellor. He played for safety and economy, with a policy of stealthy progress. His great experience and cold judgment, his powerful intellect, industry and grasp of detail made him supreme.

PLATE 22. *Painting attributed to M. Gheeraedts.* $43\frac{1}{2} \times 35\frac{1}{2}$ in. No. 362.

SIR THOMAS GRESHAM. 1519?–1579.

In the reigns of Edward VI, Mary and Elizabeth he was the adviser and agent of the government on credit, recoinage and loans. Master of exchange technique and a cosmopolitan, he restored the country to a state of financial independence. He built the first Royal Exchange and founded Gresham College.

PLATE 23. *Painting attributed to Sir A. Mor.* $38\frac{1}{2} \times 28\frac{1}{4}$ in. No. 352.

ROBERT CECIL, 1st EARL OF SALISBURY. 1563–1612.

Secretary of State and Lord High Treasurer. He contrived the succession of James I and carried over into his government the cautious policy of his own father, the great Lord Burghley. He negotiated the 1604 treaty with Spain. In 1607 he began to build Hatfield House.

PLATE 24. *Painting attributed to J. de Critz, 1602.* $35\frac{1}{2} \times 28\frac{1}{2}$ in. No. 107.

SIR RICHARD GRENVILLE. 1541?–1591.

Naval commander. In 1585 he bungled Raleigh's expedition to Virginia; he organised the West Country's defences against the threat of a Spanish Armada, and in 1591 commanded the *Revenge* in Howard's action off 'Flores in the Azores'. Buckland Abbey was his home.

PLATE 25. *Painting by an unknown artist, 1571.* $40\frac{1}{2} \times 28$ in. No. 1612.

SIR PHILIP SIDNEY. 1554–1586.

Aesthete, courtier, writer, and 'pattern of Chivalry'. Sent on several diplomatic missions, at home he was a member of the literary groups that met in Leicester House and at Wilton, the home of his sister, Lady Pembroke. Spencer was his friend. He was mortally wounded whilst fighting as a volunteer against Spain in the Low Countries. His prose works are the *Apologie for Poetrie* and the love romance *Arcadia*. His best known poetry is contained in *Astrophel and Stella*.

PLATE 26. *Painting by an unknown artist.* 45 × 32 in. No. 2096.

ROBERT DUDLEY, EARL OF LEICESTER. 1532–1588.
Soldier, politician and courtier. With his father, the Duke of Northumberland, he proclaimed Lady Jane Grey Queen; the Duke was executed. From 1558 till his death he was the favourite of Elizabeth, whom, for a period, he hoped to marry. He was opposed to Burghley on the Privy Council. Incompetently he commanded the army sent to Flanders, 1585–7.

PLATE 27. *Painting by an unknown artist.* 42 × 32 in. No. 447.

SIR FRANCIS DRAKE. 1540?–1596.
Circumnavigator, privateer and Admiral. After making three voyages to the West Indies he started on his famous voyage round the world in 1577 and reached home in 1580. Taken into government service, he was let loose on the Spanish Main in 1585 and again in 1587, and was second-in-command against the Armada. His last expedition was to the West Indies, where he died. He acquired Buckland Abbey from Grenville.

PLATE 28. *Engraving probably by Jodocus Hondius.* 15 × 12 in. No. 3905.

ROBERT DEVEREUX, 2ND EARL OF ESSEX. 1566–1601.
Stepson of Leicester, who knighted him after Zutphen and brought him to the Queen's favour, wherein he was Raleigh's rival. In 1591 he ineffectually commanded the army sent to help Henry of Navarre in France. As leader of the war party in the Council, he opposed the Cecils. He captured Cadiz (1596) and next year commanded the abortive expedition against Spain. His overweening conduct to the Queen and his failure to crush Tyrone in Ireland prefaced his attempted *coup d'état* in 1601, for which he was executed.

PLATE 29. *Painting by an unknown artist, 1597.* 24¼ × 19¼ in. No. 180.

SIR WALTER RALEIGH. 1552?–1618.
Soldier and sailor; colonist and explorer; courtier and writer. He became a favourite of Queen Elizabeth until his love affair with a

maid-of-honour brought him to imprisonment in the Tower in 1592. He spent a fortune on attempting to colonise the coast of America. In 1595 he explored Guiana, and was in high command at Cadiz (1596). On James's accession he was accused of complicity in the Arabella Stuart plot and sent to the Tower, where he began his *History of the World*. Released to find gold in Guiana, he clashed with the Spaniards, and to appease them was executed. His prose was of the first order and his lyrics were described as 'most lofty, insolent and passionate'.

PLATE 30. *Painting by an unknown artist.* 35½ × 28¾ in. No. 7.

WILLIAM SHAKESPEARE. 1564–1616.

Born and brought up at Stratford-on-Avon. He went to London about 1586, and by 1594 was well known as actor, poet and playwright, with influential patrons. In 1611 he returned to Stratford where he died. The collected edition of thirty-six plays known as the First Folio, published in 1623, had the engraving by Martin Droeshout on the title page and included the verse by Ben Jonson: this and the much-restored bust on his monument at Stratford are the only certain portraits of Shakespeare.

PLATE 31. *Engraving by Martin Droeshout, 1623.* 7½ × 6¼ in. No. 185.

BENJAMIN JONSON. 1572 or 3–1637

Every Man in his Humour (1598), in which Shakespeare played, *Volpone* and *The Alchemist* (1610) rank Jonson as the greatest English satiric dramatist. His *Epigrams*, the songs interspersed throughout his plays and masques, and collections such as *Underwoods*, with their deep thought, lyric beauty and fine craftsmanship, reveal him as a great poet.

PLATE 32. *Painting by an unknown artist.* 17½ × 15 in. No. 2752.

JOHN DONNE. 1571 or 2–1631.

Though he came of a Catholic family and, as he said, had his 'first breeding and conversation with men of a suppressed and aflicted religion', he joined the Anglican church. As a brilliant and popular young man about town and the court he was described as 'not dissolute but very neat: a great visiter of ladies, a great frequenter of plays, a great writer of conceited verse'. In later life, when he was Dean of St Paul's, he was loved and venerated as a man of deep piety and vast learning, and acclaimed as a great preacher. The passion and audacious wit of his early amorous poems gave place to the strangely involved thought, and strangely combined harmony and harshness of his 'metaphysical' verses, to be followed in turn by the exalted power of exhortation, the wealth and originality of illustration, and the grand musical periods of his sermons.

PLATE 33. *Painting after I. Oliver.* $20\frac{1}{4} \times 17$ in. No. 1849.

INIGO JONES. 1573–1652.

He designed costumes and settings for the royal Whitehall masques written by Ben Jonson and others. He twice visited Italy and introduced into England the great principles of classic architecture. He designed the Queen's House, Greenwich (1617), the Banqueting House, Whitehall (1619–22), the present Marlborough House Chapel and the West Front of Old St Paul's (1634). Of over a hundred private houses attributed to him less than a dozen, of which Wilton is one, are certainly his work.

PLATE 34. *Painting after Vandyck.* $25 \times 20\frac{1}{2}$ in. No. 603.

MICHAEL DRAYTON. 1563–1631.

He wrote many historical poems and collaborated in several plays. He is best remembered for his *Poly-Olbion*, a patriotic, mythological 'description' of England; for his *Ballard of Agincourt*; his sonnets and eclogues; his *Endymion and Phoebe*; and for the long sylvan poems of which *Nymphidia* is most prized.

PLATE 35. *Painting by an unknown artist.* $23\frac{1}{4} \times 17\frac{1}{2}$ in. No. 776.

KING JAMES I. 1566–1625.

James VI of Scotland; son of Mary, Queen of Scots, and great-great-grandson of Henry VII. When a baby he succeeded to the Scottish throne on the abdication of his mother, and for some years was the sport of conflicting factions. He succeeded Elizabeth I on the English throne in 1603. Uncouth and undignified in appearance and conduct, and with a *penchant* for unpopular favourites, he was a learned pedant with an interest in religious questions which led him to preside over the conference at which the Authorised Version of the Bible was projected in 1604. His theories of kingship and his attitude towards Parliament sowed the seeds of discord: the harvest was reaped by his son.

PLATE 36. *Painting by Daniel Mytens, 1621.* $58\frac{1}{4} \times 39$ in. No. 109.

THE SOMERSET HOUSE CONFERENCE, 1604.

Plenipotentiaries from England, Spain and the Catholic Netherlands in conference at Somerset House in August, 1604. A treaty of peace and commerce was concluded between the three countries by which King

James I bound himself to give no more aid to the 'Hollanders or other enemies of the King of Spain and the Archdukes'.

PLATE 37. *Painting attributed to M. Gheeraedts, the younger.* 81 × 105½ in. No. 665. *The Englishmen, seen on the right, are Thomas Sackville, Earl of Dorset; Charles Howard, Earl of Nottingham; Charles Blount, Earl of Devonshire; Henry Howard, Earl of Northampton and Robert Cecil, Earl of Salisbury.*

ANNE OF DENMARK. 1574–1619.

Daughter of Frederick II and sister of Christian IV of Denmark, she married James VI and I in 1589. She was frivolous, vain and extravagant: she enjoyed taking part in masques at Court and patronised Ben Jonson and Inigo Jones. Her other great interests were building and hunting. She bore seven children, of whom three survived infancy.

PLATE 38. *Painting after P. van Somer.* 29½ × 24¾ in. No. 127.

ELIZABETH, QUEEN OF BOHEMIA. 1596–1662.

Daughter of James I, she was married in 1613 to Frederick V, the Elector Palatine, who in 1619 became King of Bohemia. Their cause excited romantic sympathy in England when the Austrians drove them out in 1620. Beautiful, gay and vivacious, she became known as the 'Queen of Hearts'. She lived for a time in poverty in Holland and returned to England after the Restoration. Prince Rupert was her most famous son: her daughter Sophia, wife of the Elector of Hanover, was the mother of George I.

PLATE 39. *Painting by Michael Jansz van Miereveldt.* 26½ × 23 in. No. 71.

FRANCIS BACON, BARON VERULAM AND VISCOUNT ST ALBAN. 1561–1626.

Son of Lord Keeper Bacon, nephew of Burghley, and friend of Essex. From the office of Lord High Chancellor, won by Buckingham's favour in 1619, he fell in 1621, impeached for bribery. He retired to devote himself to scientific study and writing. He propounded the inductive method of research and gave dubious precepts for self-advancement, which he truly practised. One of the great Renaissance intellectual aristocrats, he was yet dishonourable, corrupt and a toady. His *Essays, Advancement of Learning, Novum Organum* and the uncannily prophetic *New Atlantis* are the measure of his genius.

PLATE 40. *Painting from the studio of P. van Somer.* 77½ × 50 in. No. 1288.

GEORGE VILLIERS, 1st DUKE OF BUCKINGHAM. 1592–1628.

Favourite of James I and Charles I, and their evil genius. His swift rise to power was largely due to his good looks and fine manners, and by 1619 he was the virtual ruler of England. He dispensed monopolies to hangers-on, seconded Charles' attempt to woo the Spanish Infanta in 1623, was unsuccessful as a military commander, and achieved immense unpopularity. After the defeat of his expedition in aid of the Huguenots of La Rochelle he was assassinated at Portsmouth when about to return with another force.

PLATE 41. *Painting by an unknown artist.* 81 × 47 in. No. 3840.

HENRIETTA MARIA. 1609–1669.

Daughter of Henri IV of France and Marie de Medici, she was married to Charles I in 1625. She was a militant Catholic, headstrong and indomitable, and though animated by a sincere devotion to her husband her influence was fatal. In 1644 she escaped to France where she lived in poverty till the Restoration when she came to England. In 1665 she returned to France for good.

PLATE 42. *Painting by an unknown artist.* 84½ × 52½ in. No. 1247.

KING CHARLES I. 1600–1649.

Son of James I whom he succeeded in 1625. Thanks largely to the influence of his unpopular favourite, Buckingham, and later to the schemes of his Catholic wife, and to his own unyielding insistence on the Divine Right of Kings, the struggle for power between him and Parliament led to civil war and to his trial and execution. His private life was exemplary and he was an affectionate husband and father: he was a discerning connoisseur of the arts, the patron of Vandyck and Rubens, and a great collector of pictures.

PLATE 43. *Painting by Daniel Mytens, 1631.* 84½ × 52½ in. No. 1246.

THOMAS WENTWORTH, 1st EARL OF STRAFFORD. 1593–1641.

At first siding with Parliament, he was won over by Charles I who admired and respected his sincerity and honesty. In 1628 he was appointed President of the Council of the North and in 1632 Lord Deputy in Ireland, where he restored order by the institution of the policy of repression he called 'Thorough'. Convinced of the necessity for absolute authority, he returned to England in 1639 intent on the maintenance of the royal power, despite the dangerous temper of the people. Suspicions that he intended to use the Irish army against Parliament led to his arrest, attainder and execution.

PLATE 44. *Painting after Vandyck.* 50 × 42 in. No. 2960.

WILLIAM LAUD. 1573–1645.

High Churchman and Archbishop of Canterbury; leader of the Church at Charles I's accession and also prominent in secular affairs. Passionately sincere, opinionated and an inveterate foe of Puritanism, he followed Strafford's policy of 'Thorough' in ecclesiastical affairs. By enforcing ritualism and uniformity of Church Services in England he drove 20,000 refugees to America by 1640: by forcing the English pattern Prayer Book on Scotland he raised the Covenanters. At the end of 1640 he was impeached by Parliament for treason: four years later he was executed.

PLATE 45. *Painting from the studio of Vandyck.* $47\frac{1}{4} \times 36\frac{1}{4}$ in. No. 171.

OLIVER CROMWELL. 1599–1658.

He entered Parliament in 1628 and became a keen Puritan. His military genius became apparent at Edgehill, after which he formed his New Model Army, the chief single factor in winning the Civil War. After the King's execution in 1649 he defeated the Scots at Dunbar, 1650, and Charles II at Worcester, 1651. In 1653 he was declared Protector and instituted a despotic form of government by ordinance, dispensing with parliaments: he did much to retrieve England's place as a European power. He was a master of English prose and many of his sayings are memorable.

PLATE 46. *Painting by Robert Walker.* $49\frac{1}{2} \times 39\frac{1}{2}$ in. No. 536.

THOMAS HOWARD, 2ND EARL OF ARUNDEL AND SURREY. 1586–1646.

He travelled much and formed an art collection which was the finest in England in his day and included the incomparable Holbein drawings now at Windsor and the 'Arundel Marbles' now at Oxford. Patron and friend of artists and antiquaries, he was called by Horace Walpole 'the father of *Vertu* in England'. Though contributing generously in money to the Royalist cause he hated war and in 1642 he retired to Padua.

PLATE 47. *Painting by Sir Peter Paul Rubens.* $26\frac{1}{4} \times 20\frac{1}{2}$ in. No. 2391.

SIR ANTHONY VANDYCK. 1599–1641.

The most accomplished portrait painter of his day. Born at Antwerp, he became assistant to Rubens and he first visited England in 1620 on Lord Arundel's invitation. After winning fame in the Netherlands and Italy he returned at Charles I's request in 1632 and lived in London off and on till his death. He painted many royal portraits and was employed by most of the great families. His influence on English painting extended to Reynolds and Gainsborough.

PLATE 48. *Painting after a self portrait.* 24¼ × 19 in. No. 1291.

JOHN MILTON. 1608–1674.

'He can occasionally invest himself with grace' (as witness *L'Allegro*, *Il Penseroso*, *Lycidas* and the masque, *Comus*, all written before the age of thirty) 'but his natural port is gigantick loftiness. Before the greatness displayed in Milton's poem all other greatness shrinks away'. *Paradise Lost*, which won this tribute from the most captious of critics, Dr Johnson, was written after he went blind and was published in 1667; his genius was so little recognised during his lifetime that it brought him and his widow a total of only £18. It was followed by *Paradise Regained* and *Samson Agonistes*. He was a Puritan and supporter of the Commonwealth and for a time Latin Secretary to the Council of State. He engaged with vehemence in political and theological controversy, often displaying impeccable latinity but dubious reasoning and taste.

PLATE 49. *Engraving by William Faithorne, 1670.* 8½ × 6 in. No. 610.

THOMAS FAIRFAX, 3RD BARON FAIRFAX OF CAMERON. 1612–1671.

A soldier by profession, honest, modest, moderate, with no bent for politics, he fought on the side of Parliament at Marston Moor, was Commander-in-chief in 1645, and with Cromwell commanded the New Model Army. He retired after the execution of the King, which he tried hard to prevent, and only once emerged from private life to head the commission inviting Charles II to return.

PLATE 50. *Engraving by W. Faithorne after R. Walker.* 10¾ × 7½ in. No. 3624.

JOHN EVELYN. 1620–1706.

Evelyn proposed the foundation of the Royal Society, and became its secretary. He was much at Charles II's court, member of various commissions, and Treasurer of Greenwich Hospital. He was a virtuoso and a man of wide culture: his chief works are *Sculptura*, treating of the art of mezzotint, *Sylva*, a book on practical arboriculture, and *Numismata*, a discourse on medals. His invaluable *Diary* was first published in 1818.

PLATE 51. *Engraving by Robert Nanteuil*, 9½ × 6½ in. No. 3258.

SIR THOMAS BROWNE. 1605-1682.

He studied medicine at Montpellier, Padua and Leyden and settled as a doctor in Norwich. His *Religio Medici*, which reveals his philosophy and beliefs, has been described as 'a prophylactic against totalitarian damnation', and an antidote to 'Donne's dark theology'. It was translated into three languages, and with his *Vulgar Errors* and *Urn Burial* has retained its public as much for style and eloquence as for erudition.

PLATE 52. *Painting attributed to Joan Carlile*. 7 × 8¾ in. No. 2062.

THOMAS HOBBES. 1588-1679.

The first great English writer on the science of government. The cynical political theories expounded in his chief work, *Leviathan; or the Matter, Form and Power of a Commonwealth, Ecclesiastical and Civil*, published in 1651, caused some sensation. His geometrical theories earned scant respect, but as a philosopher he had great influence in England and also on foreign thinkers such as Leibniz, Spinoza and Rousseau.

PLATE 53. *Painting by John Michael Wright*. 35¼ × 27½ in. No. 225.

WILLIAM HARVEY. 1578-1657.

When Lumleian lecturer at the Royal College of Physicians in 1616 he first propounded his theory of the circulation of the blood which he published at Frankfort in 1628. He was physician to St Bartholomew's Hospital, to James I and to Charles I, whom he accompanied on his Civil War campaigns: he was reading a book during the battle of Edgehill.

PLATE 54. *Painting by an unknown artist*. 38½ × 31¼ in. No. 60.

SAMUEL BUTLER. 1612-1680.

In 1663-4 the first two parts of his mock heroic poem *Hudibras* were published and the third part followed in 1678: it had a widespread popularity. In this medley of scholarship and 'Hogarthian' humour the satire was for the most part aimed at the Puritans.

PLATE 55. *Painting by Gerard Soest*. 47¾ × 40½ in. No. 2468.

IZAAK WALTON. 1593–1683.

An ironmonger by trade, and a freeman of the company, he took to writing in his spare time. Besides poetry he wrote a life of his friend John Donne, and of Sir Henry Wotton, Richard Hooker, George Herbert, and Bishop Sanderson—this last written when he was eighty-five. His *Compleat Angler* (1653), haunted by the nature poetry of the Elizabethans and his own simplicity and goodness, is one of the best-loved books in the English language.

PLATE 56. *Painting by Jacob Huysmans.* 29¼ × 24¼ in. No. 1168.

JOHN BUNYAN. 1628–1688.

A tinker by trade he became a travelling preacher; imprisoned in 1660 as unlicensed, he began writing. Again imprisoned in 1675 in the bridge-house, Bedford, he there composed *Pilgrim's Progress*, which came to 'represent religion to thousands of the poor'. Apart from its spiritual significance it has great narrative craftsmanship.

PLATE 57. *Painting by Thomas Sadler, 1684.* 29 × 24 in. No. 1311.

SIR PETER LELY. 1618–1680.

Born in Westphalia of Dutch parents, he came to England in 1641 and succeeded Vandyck as principal portrait painter. His 'Admirals' of the Dutch Wars, now at Greenwich, and his 'Windsor Beauties', at Hampton Court, represent him well. Immeasurably he out-distanced all rivals, but his popularity led him to employ many assistants whose work, with that of his imitators, is often attributed to him.

PLATE 58. *Painting by himself.* 44½ × 36¼ in. No. 3897.

PRINCE RUPERT, COUNT PALATINE. 1619–1682.

Son of Elizabeth, Queen of Bohemia, and nephew of Charles I. Regarded as the typical Cavalier, he was a brilliant cavalry leader and fought with reckless valour in the Civil War, but was defeated at Marston Moor and Naseby. From 1648 to 1652 he fought the Parliamentary forces at sea, and after the Restoration continued his naval career as an admiral in the wars against the Dutch. In 1670 he founded the Hudson Bay Company for the exploration of North America. He was interested in scientific experiment and was a pioneer of mezzo-tint engraving.

PLATE 59. *Painting by or after Lely.* 41½ × 31½ in. No. 608.

KING CHARLES II. 1630–1685.

Proclaimed King in Scotland after his father's execution, he invaded England in an attempt to regain the throne: after his defeat at Worcester in 1651 he escaped to the Continent and was in exile till restored to the throne amid general rejoicing in 1660. His self-indulgence and dissimulation were offset by his talent for yielding to the pressure of events at the right moment, and despite the many difficulties and dangers of his reign he succeeded in retaining the throne till his death. His accessibility and tolerant good humour made him popular with his people. He was an enthusiastic amateur of science and chemistry and was the first patron of the Royal Society whose meetings he often attended.

PLATE 60. *Painting attributed to J. M. Wright.* $49\frac{1}{2} \times 39\frac{1}{2}$ in. No. 531.

CATHERINE OF BRAGANZA. 1638–1705.

Daughter of John IV of Portugal: she was married to Charles II in 1662 bringing as her dowry Bombay and Tangier. Evelyn noted her pretty shape, 'languishing and excellent eyes' and projecting teeth. There were no children of the marriage. Assailed during the Popish Plot, she was steadfastly protected by the King who, in spite of his infidelities, had much affection for her. She returned to Portugal in 1692 and was Regent during the illness of her brother, Pedro II.

PLATE 61. *Painting by Dirk Stoop.* 48×39 in. No. 2563.

ELEANOR (NELL) GWYN. 1650–1687.

As a child she sold oranges in the pit at Drury Lane theatre, and later was an actress there and at Dorset Gardens. About 1668 she became one of Charles II's mistresses. Her gaiety, good temper and cockney wit greatly appealed to him and she kept his favour till his death. One of their sons was created Duke of St Albans.

PLATE 62. *Engraving by G. Valck after Lely.* $12\frac{1}{2} \times 10$ in. No. 3811.

LOUISE RENÉE DE PENENCOUET DE KEROUALLE, DUCHESS OF PORTSMOUTH. 1649–1734.

She attended the Duchess of Orleans on her visit to Dover in 1670 and later returned to England and became the King's mistress: their son was created Duke of Richmond. She used her 'childish, simple, baby face' so well that her rooms in Whitehall were ten times as rich as the Queen's. The belief that she exerted all her influence in the French and Catholic interest made her widely distrusted and detested.

PLATE 63. *Painting by Pierre Mignard, 1682.* $47\frac{1}{2} \times 37\frac{1}{2}$ in. No. 497.

GEORGE MONCK, 1st DUKE OF ALBEMARLE. 1608–1670.

Taken prisoner at Nantwich when fighting for Charles I, he went over to the Parliamentarians. Under Cromwell he was in command in Ireland and later in Scotland. After Cromwell's death he supported Parliament against the Army party. In 1660 he marched from Scotland to London, secured the election of the Convention parliament, welcomed Charles II back to the throne and was made a Duke. He courageously stayed in London to maintain order and organise relief during the Great Plague of 1665. He fought as an admiral in the Dutch Wars.

PLATE 64. *Painting from the studio of Lely.* 49 × 39½. No. 423.

EDWARD HYDE, 1st EARL OF CLARENDON. 1609–1674.

Originally an opponent of the Court, he went over to Charles I, urging in vain a legal constitutional attitude. He was Charles II's chief adviser during the exile and after the Restoration. Between 1661 and 1665 the five penal laws in support of Anglicanism known as the Clarendon Code were passed and rigorously enforced. His overweening pride made him universally unpopular and his dictatorial manner alienated the King; he was blamed for all the disasters of the time, was impeached in 1667 and, no longer able to rely on the King's protection, fled to France. There he finished his great *History of the Rebellion* begun during the exile.

PLATE 65. *Painting after A. Hanneman.* 35½ × 28½ in. No. 773.

HENRIETTA ANNE, DUCHESS OF ORLEANS. 1644–1670.

Charles II's youngest and favourite sister. Born at Exeter, she was smuggled to France in 1646 and brought up by her mother as a strict Catholic. In 1661 she was married to Louis XIV's unpleasant brother, Philippe, Duke of Orleans. She was the trusted intermediary between Charles II and Louis XIV in the negotiations that led up to the secret Treaty of Dover in 1670. The unhappiness of her marriage led many at the time to believe that her sudden death was due to poison.

PLATE 66. *Painting by an unknown artist.* 31 × 24½ in. No. 228.

JOHN MAITLAND, 1st DUKE OF LAUDERDALE. 1616–1682.

He obtained Charles II's nominal acceptance of the Scottish Covenant in 1650. Captured at the battle of Worcester he was nine years in prison. As Secretary of State for Scotland at the Restoration he harshly and persistently tried to impose the absolute power of the King in Church and State. He was a member of the 'Cabal' ministry.

PLATE 67. *Painting by an unknown artist.* 49½ × 38 in. No. 2084.

ANTHONY ASHLEY-COOPER, 1st EARL OF SHAFTESBURY. 1621–1683.

Supported Charles I till 1644 when he joined the Parliamentarians; one of the commissioners to recall Charles II; he became Chancellor of the Exchequer in 1661 and Lord Chancellor in 1672. He was one of the 'Cabal' ministry, and he was satirised by Dryden as Achitophel A rigid anti-Catholic, his 'Green Ribbon Club' was the headquarters of the Whig exclusionist party where the technique of rabble-raising was exploited. His schemes for insurrection in support of Monmouth as heir to the throne failing, he fled to Amsterdam where he died.

PLATE 68. *Painting after J. Greenhill.* 49½ × 39¼. No. 3893.

SIR WILLIAM TEMPLE, BART. 1628–1699.

He married Dorothy Osborne in 1655 after a long engagement during which her famous letters to him were written. Under Charles II he was sent on various diplomatic missions, and as ambassador at The Hague he forwarded the marriage of Princess Mary to William of Orange. He was a disinterested patriot, but his efforts meeting with indifferent success he retired to his country houses and his writing. He is considered one of the best essayists of his time: Johnson admired his cadence.

PLATE 69. *Painting attributed to Lely.* 28¼ × 23½ in. No. 152.

SAMUEL PEPYS. 1632/3–1703.

His *Diary* of the years 1660 to 1669, which was not intended for publication and was written in code, was first deciphered and published in 1825. Both as a precise record of Restoration England and as a human document it is unsurpassed: despite the picture of himself as an amiable and slightly absurd little man which emerges from it, he was a thoroughly efficient administrator and reformer at the Admiralty. A bibliophil, a connoisseur and a musician, he was interested in most of the arts and sciences and was President of the Royal Society in 1685.

PLATE 70. *Painting by John Hayls, 1666.* 29½ × 24¼ in. No. 211.

ANNA MARIA TALBOT, COUNTESS OF SHREWSBURY (NÉE BRUDENELL). DIED 1702.

Second wife of Francis, 11th Earl of Shrewsbury, whom she married in 1659. After several discreditable amorous intrigues she became the mistress of the 2nd Duke of Buckingham and is supposed to have assisted, disguised as a page, at the duel in which her husband was killed by her lover. Later she married a Mr Bridges.

PLATE 71. *Painting by Sir Peter Lely.* $29\frac{1}{4} \times 24$ in. No. 280.

GEORGE VILLIERS, 2ND DUKE OF BUCKINGHAM. 1627/8–1687.

Son of the favourite of James I and Charles I, he was brought up with Charles II and became his friend. Brilliant but unstable, profligate and malicious, he was instrumental in procuring the fall of Clarendon, and became one of the 'Cabal' ministry: on its break-up he joined Shaftesbury's Whig party. In his burlesque *The Rehearsal* he satirised Dryden, who in revenge satirised him even more effectively as Zimry in *Absalom and Achitophel*.

PLATE 72. *Painting by Sir Peter Lely.* 29×24 in. No. 279.

KING JAMES II. 1633–1701.

Second son of Charles I. As Duke of York he was a soldier of fortune in the French and Spanish armies during the exile. In the Dutch Wars after the Restoration he showed great ability as Lord High Admiral, both ashore and afloat, but as a convert to Roman Catholicism he resigned on the passing of the Test Act in 1673. His attempts to Catholicise England after his succession to the throne and, finally, the birth of a Catholic heir brought about the Revolution of 1688 and the unopposed landing of William of Orange. He fled to France and died in exile at St Germains.

PLATE 73. *Painting by Sir Godfrey Kneller, 1685.* $92\frac{3}{4} \times 56\frac{3}{4}$ in. No. 666.

ANNE, DUCHESS OF YORK (NÉE HYDE). 1637–1671.

Daughter of the Earl of Clarendon and first wife of James II to whom she was 'contracted' in Holland when she was Maid of Honour to Mary, Princess of Orange. A legal marriage took place in 1660, and she bore her husband eight children of whom two, Princesses Mary and Anne, survived and became Queens of England.

PLATE 74. *Painting from the studio of Lely.* $28\frac{1}{2} \times 24$ in. No. 241.

MARY OF MODENA. 1658–1718.

Daughter of Alfonso IV, Duke of Modena, and second wife of James II whom she married in 1673 when she was fifteen and he forty:

in spite of this disparity the marriage was a happy one. They had seven children of whom two survived infancy, Prince James Francis Edward and Princess Louisa Maria Theresa.

PLATE 75. *Painting by William Wissing.* $47\frac{1}{2} \times 38\frac{1}{2}$ in. No. 214.

GEORGE JEFFREYS, 1ST BARON JEFFREYS. 1648–1689.

Chief Justice of the King's Bench, 1682, and Lord Chancellor, 1685–8. After Monmouth's rebellion the savagery of his sentences at what came to be known as the 'Bloody Assize' made his name a byword. After the flight of James II he was imprisoned in the Tower where he died.

PLATE 76. *Painting attributed to W. P. Claret.* 49×39 in. No. 56.

JAMES SCOTT, DUKE OF MONMOUTH AND BUCCLEUGH. 1649–1685.

Son of Charles II and Lucy Walter: Charles loved him and acknowledged him, but always strenuously denied his legitimacy. He became the champion of Protestantism and the centre of Whig plots to exclude James from the succession. On the accession of James II he headed a rebellion and claimed the throne, was defeated at Sedgemoor and beheaded on Tower Hill. Evelyn's epitaph for him was 'debauched by lust, seduced by crafty knaves'.

PLATE 77. *Painting after Lely.* $48\frac{1}{2} \times 40$. No. 556.

JOHN DRYDEN. 1631–1700.

Author of nearly twenty plays, one of the best known being *All for Love*, some brilliant political satires, including *Absalom and Achitophel*, the famous odes, *St Cecilia's Day* and *Alexander's Feast*, and the great religious poems such as *The Hind and the Panther* which treats of his conversion to Catholicism. He was poet-laureate from 1670, but like many other Catholics lost office on the accession of William and Mary. He was one of our great literary critics and the first to accord Shakespeare and Milton their supreme position.

PLATE 78. *Painting by Sir Godfrey Kneller.* 49×38 in. No. 2083.

JOHN LOCKE. 1632–1704.

He published his *Essay Concerning Toleration* in 1667 and became the 1st Earl of Shaftesbury's medical attendant and secretary. Suspected of plotting with Shaftesbury in 1684 he withdrew to Holland till the

Revolution which, like later revolutions, was influenced by his ideas on Civil Government. His supreme work, *An Essay Concerning Humane Understanding*, was published in 1690.

PLATE 79. *Painting by John Greenhill*, 22½ × 18½ in. No. 3912.

HENRY PURCELL, 1658?–1695.

He was a chorister of the Chapel Royal, studying under Cooke, Humfrey and Blow, then Organist of Westminster Abbey from 1680 till his early death. He began composing as a child and excelled in religious works, songs and sonatas, operas and incidental orchestral music for plays. He composed music for a number of Dryden's plays: one of his loveliest works, the opera *Dido and Aeneas*, was written for a girls' school.

PLATE 80. *Painting attributed to John Closterman*. 29 × 24½ in. No. 1352.

SIR CHRISTOPHER WREN. 1632–1723.

His early bent was for mathematics, meteorology and astronomy; one of his first buildings was the Sheldonian Theatre, Oxford (1662). Immediately after the great fire of 1666 he produced a plan (not used) for rebuilding the City of London. Thenceforward he was incessantly busy with the City Churches, new St Paul's, the Royal works—Chelsea, Winchester, Hampton Court and Greenwich—and buildings at Oxford and Cambridge. He helped to found the Royal Society and was President from 1680 to 1682.

PLATE 81. *Painting by Sir Godfrey Kneller, 1711*. 49 × 39½ in. No. 113.

SIR ISAAC NEWTON. 1642–1727.

He worked out the binomial theorem, the differential calculus and the integral calculus in 1665, at which time the law of gravitation was also in his mind, though he did not make it known until its inclusion in the first book of his *Principia* which he showed to the Royal Society in 1686: the complete work was published the following year. Meanwhile he worked at optics and constructed two reflecting telescopes. He was President of the Royal Society for twenty-five years, and it is said that he was phenomenally absent-minded.

PLATE 82. *Painting by Sir Godfrey Kneller, 1702*. 30 × 25 in. No. 2881.

SIR GODFREY KNELLER, BART. 1646–1723.

Born at Lübeck, he came to England about 1674 and was principal portrait painter after the death of Lely in 1680. At Hampton Court is a gallery of the 'Beauties' he painted for Mary II and at Greenwich a fine series of Admirals done for William III: the portraits of the members of the Kit-Cat Club commissioned by Jacob Tonson are in the National Portrait Gallery. He amassed a fortune and built himself a sumptuous mansion: many anecdotes have survived to illustrate his inordinate conceit and complacency.

PLATE 83. *Painting by himself, 1685.* 28 × 24 in. No. 3794.

KING WILLIAM III. 1650–1702.

As grandson of Charles I and husband of James II's daughter, Mary, he had a double reversionary claim to the throne of England. He was Stadholder of Holland and he became the Protestant champion of Europe against the aggression of Louis XIV. When James II's hope of Catholicising England was strengthened by the birth of an heir in 1688, William of Orange was invited by a group of Whigs to invade England. On James's flight William and Mary were declared King and Queen on terms which swept away the old Tudor and Stuart absolutism. He defeated James's counter attacks at the Boyne and La Hogue, and formed the Grand Alliance against France. He was austere and taciturn and showed no wish for popularity.

PLATE 84. *Painting after Lely.* 48½ × 39¼ in. No. 1902.

QUEEN MARY II. 1662–1694.

Elder daughter of James II by his first wife, Anne Hyde. She married William of Orange in 1677, but bore no children. After her father's flight she came from Holland to be proclaimed joint sovereign with her husband; she came into Whitehall 'laughing and jolly'. She was wise, tactful and popular, and during William's frequent absences she ruled alone, loyally supporting him despite some neglect on his part.

PLATE 85. *Painting after W. Wissing.* 48½ × 39½ in. No. 197.

WILLIAM BENTINCK, 1st EARL OF PORTLAND. 1649–1709.

A Dutchman who was early in William III's service and negotiated his marriage with Princess Mary: he came to England with King William in 1688, was his most trusted agent for foreign affairs and was richly rewarded with honours and lands.

PLATE 86. *Painting from the studio of H. Rigaud.* 54½ × 46 in. No. 1968.

CHARLES MONTAGU, 1st EARL OF HALIFAX. 1661–1715.

As Chancellor of the Exchequer from 1692 he originated the National Debt, the Consolidated Fund, Exchequer Bills and, in 1694, established the Bank of England. Out of favour in Queen Anne's reign, he became First Lord of the Treasury on the accession of George I. In collaboration with Prior he wrote the . . . *Country Mouse and City Mouse* (1687), a parody of Dryden.

PLATE 87. *Painting by Sir Godfrey Kneller.* 49 × 39 in. No. 800.

QUEEN ANNE, 1665–1714, AND HER SON WILLIAM, DUKE OF GLOUCESTER, 1689–1700.

Second daughter of James II by his first wife, Anne Hyde. Throughout her reign she was surrounded by the strife of political factions, and the influence of her favourites, particularly the Duchess of Marlborough and, later, Mrs Masham, was the focal point of perpetual intrigues. She was steadfast in her Anglicanism and granted to the Church the revenues known as 'Queen Anne's Bounty'. Obstinacy rather than astuteness may have characterised her statesmanship, but her homely virtues won her the title of 'Good Queen Anne.' Her son William, a delicate, bright boy who survived longer than any other of her many children, was the last hope for a direct succession of Protestant sovereigns.

PLATE 88. *Painting after Kneller.* 48 × 39½ in. No. 325.

PRINCE GEORGE OF DENMARK. 1653–1708.

Son of Frederick III of Denmark and Consort of Queen Anne, whom he married in 1683. His easy good nature made him well liked by all about him and much loved by his wife. He took little part in public affairs. When Anne came to the throne in 1702 she failed to have him accepted as Captain-General of the Allied Forces or to secure for him at home the dignities of a ruling monarch: she made him Lord High Admiral with a council to conduct the administration, and, as nominal head of the navy, much of the violent criticism of mismanagement fell on him.

PLATE 89. *Painting after J. Riley.* 48½ × 39½. No. 326.

JOHN CHURCHILL, 1st DUKE OF MARLBOROUGH. 1650–1722.

As a soldier and commander of a mixed allied force from 1702 till 1711 he was superb, his most famous victories being Blenheim, Ramillies, Oudenarde, and Malplaquet: he was rewarded with Blenheim Palace and a Dukedom. The very great power he wielded at the beginning of

Queen Anne's reign gradually diminished until finally he was charged with corruption and dismissed. He was reinstated Captain General by George I.

PLATE 90. *Painting after Kneller.* $48\frac{3}{4} \times 40$ in. No. 553.

SARAH CHURCHILL, DUCHESS OF MARL-BOROUGH (NÉE JENNINGS). 1660–1744.

Appointed maid-of-honour to Princess (Queen) Anne about 1676. She and her husband were a devoted couple, and as 'Mr and Mrs Free-man' were for many years close friends of 'Mrs Morley', the Queen. Her quarrels with Queen Anne hastened Marlborough's fall. Her wit and conversation shone; when over seventy she was still the life of the hazard table at Tunbridge Wells. Her conflicts with the architect, Vanbrugh, at Blenheim were notorious.

PLATE 91. *Painting after Kneller.* $41 \times 34\frac{1}{4}$ in. No. 3634.

JAMES STANHOPE, 1ST EARL STANHOPE. 1673–1727.

He was made commander-in-chief of our forces in Spain in 1708; he took Port Mahon, annexed Minorca, and won a victory at Saragossa, but at the disaster at Brihuega in 1711 he was captured and lost all he had gained. He was active in securing the Hanoverian succession, and under George I was First Lord of the Treasury and a most capable Foreign Minister.

PLATE 92. *Painting by Sir Godfrey Kneller.* 36×28 in. No. 3225.

SIR GEORGE ROOKE. 1650–1709.

Admiral. His failure at Cadiz in 1702 was atoned when he destroyed a Franco-Spanish fleet in Vigo Bay, and was erased in 1704 by his capture of Gibraltar and by his engagement against heavy odds of the French fleet off Malaga. In his day as famous at sea as Marlborough was on land, he also lost his command in the turmoil of political intrigue.

PLATE 93. *Painting by Michael Dahl.* 28×23 in. No. 1992.

WILLIAM DAMPIER. 1652–1715.

He was engaged in any number of piratical expeditions under various buccaneering captains. Under official auspices he commanded expeditions to the South Pacific in 1699–1700, coasting North Australia and New Guinea, and again in 1703. During a life that was wildly adventurous even for those times, he recorded his observations in a diary; he published his *Voyage Round the World* in 1697 and his valuable treatise, *Discourse of Winds*, in 1699.

PLATE 94. *Painting by Thomas Murray.* 29×24 in. No. 538.

HENRY ST JOHN, 1st VISCOUNT BOLINGBROKE. 1678–1751.

Secretary at War, 1704–8, and Secretary of State, 1710, in Harley's cabinet. He negotiated the Treaty of Utrecht, 1713; he also treated privately with the Pretender. On the accession of George I he was dismissed, and fled to France. He was later pardoned, but still spent much of his time abroad. He was a brilliant orator and converser, and he wrote on politics, history and philosophy. His *Patriot King* greatly influenced George III.

PLATE 95. *Painting by an unknown artist.* 57 × 44 in. No. 593.

ROBERT HARLEY, 1st EARL OF OXFORD AND MORTIMER. 1661–1724.

He helped to bring in William III and after holding many high offices headed a Tory ministry in 1710, when he dismissed Marlborough but was ousted from leadership by Bolingbroke. On the accession of George I he was impeached and confined in the Tower: tried and acquitted, he still kept a foot in each camp—Jacobite and Hanoverian. He and his son collected the Harleian Library now in the British Museum.

PLATE 96. *Painting after Kneller.* 49 × 39 in. No. 16.

JACOB TONSON. 1656?–1736.

Publisher of Milton and Dryden, Addison and Steele, Rowe's edition of *Shakespeare*, and *The Spectator*. Pope's *Shakespeare* was published for Tonson's benefit. He was secretary of the Kit-Cat Club and commissioned Kneller to paint the portraits of the members which are now in the National Portrait Gallery.

PLATE 97. *Painting by Sir Godfrey Kneller, 1717.* 36 × 28 in. No. 3230.

SIR JOHN VANBRUGH. 1664–1726.

The author of two original plays, *The Relapse* and *The Provok'd Wife* (1696–7), and of many adaptations. In 1699 he emerged as an architect, and a master of the English Baroque, with the design for Castle Howard (1701–12), in which Hawksmoor helped; he also designed Blenheim Palace (1705–24), which Hawksmoor finished, and Seaton Delaval which was his last work. In 1704 he became Clarenceux Herald.

PLATE 98. *Painting by Sir Godfrey Kneller.* 36 × 28 in. No. 3231.

JOSEPH ADDISON. 1672–1719.

An excellent classical scholar, and able administrator and an effective political pamphleteer. He owes his fame to his mastery of the periodical essay, a form he perfected in the pages of *The Tatler*, *The Spectator* and *The Guardian*. His dramatic tragedy *Cato* (1713) was a great success.

PLATE 99. *Painting by Sir Godfrey Kneller*. 36 × 28 in. No. 3193.

SIR RICHARD STEELE. 1672–1729.

In 1709 his career as essayist was launched in his periodical *The Tatler*, for which he wrote 188 papers, collaborating with Addison. In this and *The Spectator* (1711–12) they brought the periodical essay to its height, and played a great part in restoring manners—and morality—after the license of the Restoration. His last play, *The Conscious Lovers*, was considered the best sentimental comedy of its generation.

PLATE 100. *Painting by Sir Godfrey Kneller, 1711.* 36 × 28 in. No. 3227.

JONATHAN SWIFT. 1667–1745.

Dean of St Patrick's, Dublin. With *The Tale of a Tub* and *The Battle of the Books*, he became the most effective satirist of his time. The *Journal to Stella* (Esther Johnson) has a more lasting appeal, with its informal picture of London life, its glimpses behind the curtain of politics, and its private, ageless fun: *Gulliver's Travels* delights children as a story and impresses their elders as an allegory of far-reaching implications.

PLATE 101. *Painting by Charles Jervas.* 48½ × 38¼ in. No. 278.

WILLIAM CONGREVE. 1669/70–1729.

His five plays were all written by the time he was thirty years of age. The first, *The Old Bachelor*, produced at Drury Lane in 1692/3, was immediately successful and was soon followed by *The Double Dealer* which, though not quite so popular, firmly established his reputation as the leading dramatist and worthy successor of his friend, Dryden. *Love for Love* was produced in 1695 and *The Mourning Bride* in 1697, both popular successes, the latter despite previous predictions that he would fail in tragedy. Finally in 1700 came *The Way of the World*, the most meticulously wrought and gaily sparkling of them all, in which he surpassed himself in the brilliant diction of his duels—or duets—of wit, though at the time it failed to hit the public taste: it was said to be 'too Keen a Satyr'.

PLATE 102. *Painting by Sir Godfrey Kneller.* 28½ × 24 in. No. 67.

DANIEL DEFOE. 1660 or 61–1731.

Defoe's variety is endless; as pamphleteer and essayist, there is hardly a subject he passed by; his industry and rate of output were phenomenal: his pioneer newspaper, *The Review* (1704–13), was written almost single-handed. He was nearly sixty when he wrote *Robinson Crusoe*, a masterpiece of imagination. The same vivid sympathy informs the totally different *Moll Flanders* and the *Journal of the Plague Year*.

PLATE 103. *Engraving by M. van der Gucht after J. Taverner.* $10\frac{3}{4}$ × $7\frac{1}{4}$ in. No. 3960

MATTHEW PRIOR. 1664–1721.

He became famous with his poem . . . *Country Mouse and City Mouse*, written in collaboration with Halifax to burlesque Dryden. As diplomatist he helped to negotiate the peace of Ryswick and the treaty of Utrecht. Most of his work is animated by the light and frivolous spirit seen in *The Secretary*, the poems to Chloe, his epigrams and his verses to children. He himself set greater store by his philosophical poems.

PLATE 104. *Painting by T. Hudson after J. Richardson.* $39\frac{1}{2}$ × 33 in. No. 562.

MICHAEL DAHL. 1656–1743.

Swedish potrait painter who settled in London in 1688. An easy and accomplished painter, he was Kneller's rival. Like him, he painted several of the Admirals (now at Greenwich) and a set of 'Beauties' (now at Petworth). He vainly hoped to succeed Kneller as King's Painter.

PLATE 105. *Painting by himself, 1691.* 49 × 39 in. No. 3822.

KING GEORGE I. 1660–1727.

Elector of Hanover, and great-grandson of James I. He played an important part, military and political, in Europe but remained discreetly aloof from affairs in England until he succeeded Queen Anne in 1714. He brought no Queen, having divorced his wife and confined her in a castle near Celle, and the rapacity of his German mistresses and followers added to his great unpopularity. He was unattractive and without kingly graces, but he had courage, coolness and sagacity, and he adapted himself to the British system of constitutional government which gained in strength under him. He never learnt to speak English and he died on one of his frequent journeys to Hanover.

PLATE 106. *Painting from the studio of Kneller.* $75\frac{1}{4}$ × 53 in. No. 544.

PRINCE JAMES FRANCIS EDWARD STUART, 1688–1766, AND PRINCESS LOUISA MARIA THERESA STUART, 1692–1712.

Children of James II by his second wife, Mary of Modena: they were brought up as Roman Catholics. Prince James—variously styled Prince of Wales, James III and the Chevalier de St George by his adherents, but generally known as the 'Old Pretender'—was in exile with his parents from the age of six months. He landed at Peterhead to lead the rebellion of 1715, but was pessimistic, very soon lost heart, and left. He died in Rome.

PLATE 107. *Painting by Nicolas de Largillierre, 1695.* 75 × 56½ in. No. 976.

JONATHAN RICHARDSON. 1665–1745.

A sound academic portrait painter with a large middle-class practice, more sensitive as draughtsman than as painter, and a discerning collector of pictures. He was the pupil and successor of John Riley and the teacher of Hudson, who in turn taught Reynolds. Author of *The Theory of Painting* (1715) and of poetry and literary criticism.

PLATE 108. *Painting by himself.* 29 × 24 in. No. 706.

GEORGE VERTUE. 1684–1756.

Antiquary and engraver. About 350 engraved portraits by him are known, of good, solid craftsmanship. But far more precious are his note-books—some forty of them—containing a profusion of notes and jottings for a 'History of the Art of Painting and Sculpture in England', and also much archaeological data. He never wrote the book, but the notes are the foundation of all history of British art before 1750, and were used for the *Anecdotes of Painting* by Horace Walpole who wrote 'The indefatigable pains of Mr Vertue left nothing unexplored that could illumine his subject'.

PLATE 109. *Painting by Jonathan Richardson, 1738.* 29½ × 24¼ in. No. 576.

COLLEY CIBBER. 1671–1757.

Though 'sentimental' comedy did not begin with him, he used it most successfully. His reform of erring husbands by long-suffering wives touched a new sentiment. A new 'line' in fops, played by himself, was a hit too. His best play, perhaps, is *The Careless Husband*. He was made poet laureate in 1730.

PLATE 110. *Coloured plaster bust attributed to L. F. Roubiliac.* 24½ in. high. No. 1045.

ALEXANDER POPE. 1688–1744.

His *Rape of the Lock* (1714), probably the best mock-heroic poem in the language, presents the most pleasant of Pope's facets. His *Essay on Man* (1732–4) was to 'Vindicate the ways of God to man'; his satires express man's hatred of man in unbridled, psychopathic excess. His translation of the *Iliad* (1713–20) brought him fortune as well as fame.

PLATE 111. *Pastel attributed to W. Hoare.* 28½ × 17½ in. No. 299.

SIR HANS SLOANE, BART. 1660–1753.

A successful court physician and an experimental scientist, he founded the Botanic Gardens in Chelsea and published the *Natural History of Jamaica*. His collections, library and manuscripts were the nucleus of the British Museum.

PLATE 112. *Painting by Stephen Slaughter, 1736.* 48½ × 39½ in. No. 569.

GEORGE BERKELEY. 1685–1753.

Philosopher and Bishop of Cloyne. In his philosophical writings he extended John Locke's speculations towards those of David Hume, expounding in his *Principles of Human Knowledge* the theory 'esse est percipi'. He made an abortive attempt to found a missionary college in Bermuda.

PLATE 113. *Painting by John Smibert, 1725.* 39½ × 29½ in. No. 653.

GEORGE FREDERICK HANDEL. 1685–1759.

A German, he came to England as a composer of Italian opera, which he firmly planted in London. He wrote in England thirty-six operas, of which the first, *Rinaldo*, had unprecedented success. He is best remembered for *The Water Music* (1715), *Zadok the Priest*, composed for George II's coronation, and the oratorios *Saul* (1730), *The Messiah* (1742), and *Jephtha* (1750).

PLATE 114. *Painting from the studio of T. Hudson, 1756.* 48½ × 39 in. No. 8.

ISAAC WATTS. 1674–1748.

A dissenting minister, he wrote the words of about 600 hymns, some of them our finest and most loved, for example *O God our help in ages past* and *When I survey the wondrous Cross*. He was the author of *Logic*, a popular text-book, and many other doctrinal and educational works.

PLATE 115. *Painting by an unknown artist.* 29¼ × 24½ in. No. 264.

JAMES GIBBS. 1682–1754.

An architect, his best-known church is St Martin's-in-the-Fields which influenced a century of church building here and in New England. His other works include the Radcliffe Camera, Oxford, and the Senate House, Cambridge.

PLATE 116. *Painting by John Michael Williams.* $35\frac{1}{2} \times 27$ in. No. 504.

KING GEORGE II. 1683–1760.

Son of George I, whom he succeeded in 1727. He fought valiantly under Marlborough at Oudenarde: on the death of Queen Anne he came to England with his father, with whom he was always on the worst possible terms. He was extremely bellicose and he led the British Army in person at Dettingen. His reign ended in a blaze of naval and military victories for England. Since he was not very clever and inordinately vain he was an easy tool: he was much influenced by the Queen to whom he was deeply attached despite his blatant infidelities.

PLATE 117. *Painting by Thomas Hudson.* $93 \times 56\frac{3}{4}$ in. No. 670.

CAROLINE OF BRANDENBURG-ANSPACH. 1683–1737.

Daughter of John, Margrave of Brandenburg-Anspach, she married George II in 1705 and proved one of the best Queens England has had. To her political sagacity, her tactful management of her husband and her loyalty to Walpole, much of the early success of the reign was due.

PLATE 118. *Painting from the studio of C. Jervas.* $86 \times 50\frac{1}{2}$ in. No. 369.

AUGUSTA OF SAXE-GOTHA, PRINCESS OF WALES. 1719–1772.

Daughter of Frederick II of Saxe-Gotha, she married Frederick Lewis, Prince of Wales, in 1736, and bore him nine children, of whom the second became George III. After Frederick's death, she kept up a rival court with Bute as her intimate adviser. After her death her effects 'even to her Thimble' were sold at auction.

PLATE 119. *Painting by Charles Philips, 1736.* $49 \times 39\frac{1}{2}$ in. No. 2093.

FREDERICK LEWIS, PRINCE OF WALES. 1707–1751.

Son of George II and father of George III. He kept up a feud with his parents and only on her death-bed did Queen Caroline forgive him. His court was the rallying point of opposition politicians. He took a keen interest in art and in collecting works of art.

PLATE 120. *Painting by Philip Mercier.* 48×38 in. No. 2501.

PRINCE CHARLES EDWARD LOUIS PHILIP CASIMIR STUART. 1720–1788.

The 'Young Pretender', grandson of James II. Immortal as 'Bonnie Prince Charlie', he was the hero of the 1745 rising which ended at Culloden on 16 April 1746. Thereafter the deterioration of his character alienated Jacobite sympathies. Aged fifty-two he married Louisa van Stolberg, aged nineteen, who soon left him. No vestige of glamour haloed Prince Charlie's end.

PLATE 121. *Painting by Antonio David.* $24\frac{1}{2} \times 18\frac{1}{4}$ in. No. 434.

GEORGE WADE. 1673–1748.

Field-Marshal. Famed for the military roads he built in the Highlands between 1726 and 1733. In 1745 he was despatched against the Young Pretender, who slipped by him in Yorkshire, whereupon he was superseded in his command by the Duke of Cumberland.

PLATE 122. *Painting attributed to J. van Diest.* $29\frac{1}{2} \times 24$ in. No. 1594.

DUNCAN FORBES OF CULLODEN. 1685–1747.

Scottish statesman—'greatest and best of the eighteenth century'—and Lord President of the Court of Sessions. He fought against the Old and the Young Pretender; nevertheless, after both rebellions he protested against the severity of the punitive measures. After 1715 he largely directed the destinies of Scotland with justice, wisdom and courage. 'Butcher' Cumberland spoke of him as 'that old woman who talked to me about humanity'.

PLATE 123. *After a painting attributed to J. Davison.* $29\frac{1}{2} \times 24$ in. No. 61.

WILLIAM AUGUSTUS, DUKE OF CUMBERLAND. 1721–1765.

Third son of George II. He succeeded Wade in command against the Young Pretender's army, defeated it at Culloden in 1746 and was granted an annuity of £25,000 by a grateful Parliament: by his subsequent treatment of the Highlanders he earned the title of 'Butcher'. Success did not attend the campaigns on the Continent under his command.

PLATE 124. *Painting from the studio of Reynolds.* $29\frac{1}{2} \times 24\frac{1}{2}$ in. No. 625.

ROBERT WALPOLE, 1ST EARL OF ORFORD. 1676–1745.

On his financial record he rode into power in the surf of the South Sea Scandal, and there remained for twenty-one years, 1721–42. His policy was to keep in power at any price, to keep out of war if possible, to secure the Hanoverian succession, and build up national prosperity. But for the defeat of his Excise Bill he triumphed at home: he was forced to declare war on Spain in 1730. He built Houghton and collected a famous gallery of pictures.

PLATE 125. *Painting from the studio of J. B. van Loo.* $48\frac{1}{2} \times 39\frac{1}{4}$ in. No. 70.

JOHN CARTERET, 2ND EARL GRANVILLE. 1690–1763.

Successful ambassador to Sweden and a Secretary of State in Walpole's 1721 ministry. By his charm, his grasp of European politics, and his fluency in French and German he won George I's favour, but incurred the jealousy of Townshend and Walpole and was sent to Ireland as Lord Lieutenant, 1724–30. He led the Opposition in the Lords from 1730 till Walpole's fall. Lord President of the Council, 1751–63.

PLATE 126. *Painting by William Hoare.* $49 \times 39\frac{3}{4}$ in. No. 1778.

GEORGE ANSON, 1ST BARON ANSON. 1697–1762.

Admiral. His most famous exploit was his voyage round the world, 1740–4, in command of a squadron against Spain. He returned with one ship and £500,000 of Spanish treasure. In 1747 he beat the French off Cape Finisterre. He initiated reforms in naval administration.

PLATE 127. *Painting after Reynolds.* $49\frac{3}{4} \times 39\frac{1}{2}$ in. No. 518.

EDWARD VERNON. 1684–1757.

Admiral. At the beginning of the Spanish War he captured Porto Bello, and joined in the expeditions against Cartagena, Cuba and Panama. Too vocal on the subject of naval abuses he was dismissed the service. His nickname was 'Grog': he was exceptional in caring for his men and the watered down spirits he favoured for their drink was called after him.

PLATE 128. *Painting by Thomas Gainsborough.* $48\frac{3}{4} \times 39\frac{3}{4}$ in. No. 881.

ROBERT CLIVE, 1ST BARON CLIVE. 1725–1774.

By skilful use of Sepoys he transformed the trading stations of the East India Company into an Empire. Under Stringer Lawrence against the French leader, Dupleix, he held Arcot, and relieved Trichinopoly. After the 'Black Hole' episode he re-captured Calcutta from Seraja Daula and won the great victory of Plassey (1757) with 3000 men pitted against 50,000. As Governor of Bengal (1765–6) he concentrated on administration and the reform of abuses.

PLATE 129. *Painting by Nathaniel Dance.* $49\frac{1}{2} \times 39\frac{1}{2}$ in. No. 39.

JEFFREY AMHERST, 1st BARON AMHERST. 1717–1797.

Field-Marshal. In 1758 he commanded the expedition against the French in Canada. Added to Wolfe's achievement, his victories at Louisburg and Fort Du Quesne, and the capture of Montreal, secured Canada to the Empire.

PLATE 130. *Painting by Thomas Gainsborough.* $27\frac{1}{2} \times 22\frac{1}{4}$ in. No. 150.

STRINGER LAWRENCE. 1697–1775.

'Father of the Indian Army.' In command of the East India Company's troops he established military discipline and prepared the ground for Clive who served under him at Arcot and Trichinopoly. As commander of Fort St George he withstood a long siege in 1758–9.

PLATE 131. *Painting by Thomas Gainsborough.* $29\frac{1}{4} \times 24\frac{1}{4}$ in. No. 777.

WILLIAM PULTENEY, 1st EARL OF BATH. 1684–1764.

Effective as pamphleteer, outstanding as orator, in coalition with Bolingbroke and Wyndham he harrassed Walpole in *The Craftsman* and in Parliament from 1721 till Walpole fell in 1742. He was then made Earl of Bath, but held no important office.

PLATE 132. *Painting by Sir Joshua Reynolds, 1761.* 60 × 58 in. No. 337.

RICHARD TEMPLE, 1st VISCOUNT COBHAM. 1675–1749.

As Colonel in Marlborough's campaigns he distinguished himself at Lille and took Vigo in 1719. In the House of Lords he conspired against Walpole's Excise Bill and was deprived of his military rank: on Walpole's fall he was made Field-Marshal. 'Cobham's Cubs' in Parliament included Pitt, Grenville and Lyttleton. The first of Pope's *Moral Essays* was addressed to Cobham, who was a patron of arts and letters and who rebuilt Stowe and there laid out the most famous of English landscape gardens, with its statues, obelisks, temples and summer-houses designed by Vanbrugh, Kent and Gibbs.

PLATE 133. *Painting by Jean Baptiste van Loo.* $29 \times 24\frac{1}{2}$ in. No. 286.

PHILIP DORMER STANHOPE, 4TH EARL OF CHESTERFIELD. 1694–1773.

A Whig grandee who turned against Walpole in parliament and the press. He served as Ambassador to The Hague, as Lord Lieutenant of Ireland and as a pacifically minded Secretary of State. A patron of letters and learning, he is now best known for the letters of worldly advice to his natural son and to his godson, which were not intended for publication. He built Chesterfield House, Mayfair, which was pulled down in the twentieth century, and Chesterfield House, Blackheath: in both he had a fine collection of pictures.

PLATE 134. *Painting by Allan Ramsay, 1765.* 28½ × 23½ in. No. 533.

WILLIAM PITT, 1ST EARL OF CHATHAM. 1708–1778.

'The Great Commoner' who was called to power early in the Seven Years War and organised victory by subsidising allies, selecting brilliant young commanders, and reforming the administration. At the Peace of Paris (1763), Canada and large areas of India were added to the British realm. His attitude towards the restive American colonies was liberal and he made his dying speech protesting against forceful tactics.

PLATE 135. *Painting from the studio of R. Brompton.* 45 × 33 in. No. 259.

THOMAS PELHAM-HOLLES, 1ST DUKE OF NEWCASTLE. 1693–1768.

A statesman with an enormous appetite for work, he has been called a 'master of political corruption' in that he devoted himself to accumulating compliant voters. He held a variety of offices, and as Prime Minister was responsible for the disastrous opening to the Seven Years War, which was retrieved by Chatham with whom he formed an uneasy coalition, broken by the 'King's Friends'.

PLATE 136. *Pastel by William Hoare.* 23¼ × 17½ in. No. 757.

JAMES WOLFE. 1726/7–1759.

Major-General. He fought at Dettingen and Culloden, and under Lord Amherst was prominent in the capture of Louisbourg. Lord Chatham picked him to command the expedition against the French in Canada. He was mortally wounded after his brilliant storming of the strongly held Plains of Abraham which resulted in the capture of Quebec, and died in the moment of victory: his opponent, Montcalm, was also killed.

PLATE 137. *Painting by J. S. C. Schaak.* 21 × 16½ in. No. 48.

MARGARET WOFFINGTON. 1714?–1760.

From the Dublin stage 'Peg' came to Covent Garden in 1740. She combined beauty, vivacity and ready wit, and in men's parts, such as

Harry Wildair, she was the rage: a contemporary impromptu verse says: 'Oft have I viewed theatric Peg, Unveil to sight her taper leg.' She was stricken with paralysis while playing Rosalind in 1757.

PLATE 138. *Painting by Arthur Pond.* 35 × 42 in. No. 650.

TOBIAS GEORGE SMOLLETT. 1721–1771.

His first novel, *Roderick Random* (1748), in part autobiographical, is savagely realistic in its study of life at sea, and almost burlesque in its characterisation. The same vividness of detail and caricature informs *Peregrine Pickle* (1751). *Humphry Clinker* (1771) is his masterpiece, displaying great skill in the epistolary device of narrative. He also wrote a popular *History of England*.

PLATE 139. *Painting by an unknown artist.* 27 × 20 in. No. 1110.

CATHERINE MARIA (KITTY) FISHER. Died 1767.

Famous courtesan of German parentage noted for wit as well as good looks. Her eyes, Mrs Thrale observed, were a 'species quite apart—skyblue, like a ribbon'. She married, in 1766, John Norris of Benenden.

PLATE 140. *Painting by Nathaniel Hone, 1765.* 29¼ × 24¼ in. No. 2354.

WILLIAM HOGARTH. 1697–1764.

Painter of portraits and satirical *genre*. By his choice of subject and his lusty, burlesque treatment he caught the public taste aptly with his series of paintings, *The Harlot's Progress* and *The Rake's Progress*: his combination of moralising, crude satire and unflinching realism was timely. His relation to, and influence on, the theatre and the novel of his generation makes an interesting study. His finest portrait, 'Captain Coram', his 'Shrimp Girl' and his *genre* place him with the great masters of painting.

PLATE 141. *Terra-cotta bust by Louis François Roubiliac.* 29 in. high. No. 121.

SAMUEL RICHARDSON. 1689–1761.

His *Pamela*, published in 1740, has been called the first modern novel and was extravagantly praised by contemporaries, including Dr Johnson who stressed his knowledge of the human heart. Diderot placed him beside Homer and Euripedes. There followed *Clarissa*, regarded as his best novel, and *Sir Charles Grandison*. Hogarth was engaged to illustrate *Pamela* but, possibly because his interpretation disagreed with Richardson's, the matter dropped.

PLATE 142. *Painting by Joseph Highmore, 1750.* 20 × 13¾ in. No. 1036.

GEORGE WHITEFIELD. 1714–1770.
Acquainted with the Wesleys at Oxford, he joined their group of
Methodists in 1733. Ordained deacon in 1736 and priest in 1738, his
preaching immediately produced an extraordinary popular impression.
As a Calvinistic methodist he parted company in 1741 with the
Arminian Wesley. Constantly travelling, he died in Massachusetts
on his seventh visit to America.
PLATE 143. *Painting by John Wollaston.* $31\frac{1}{2} \times 25$ in. No. 131.

JOHN WESLEY. 1703–1791.
Founder of Methodism and a scholar. While a fellow of Lincoln
College, Oxford, with his brother and others he started preaching to
prisoners and undergraduates. During some fifty years, till he was
eighty-seven, he travelled 4500 miles each year and preached thrice a
day—to miners, factory hands, fisherfolk and country folk, cheerfully
facing persecution, riots and mobbing: he eventually founded a
separate church. His literary output was prodigious.
PLATE 144. *Painting by Nathaniel Hone, 1766.* $49\frac{1}{4} \times 39\frac{1}{4}$ in. No. 135.

CHARLOTTE OF MECKLENBURG-STRELITZ.
1744–1818.
Daughter of Charles, Duke of Mecklenburg-Strelitz. She married
George III in 1761, and bore fifteen children. She was an amateur
artist, and interested in the new Royal Academy. A woman of high
principles, she faced her many sorrows with fortitude.
PLATE 145. *Painting from the studio of A. Ramsay.* 58×42 in.
No. 224.

KING GEORGE III. 1738–1820.
Grandson of George II whom he succeeded in 1760, and the first
English-born Hanoverian sovereign. Like the Stuarts he had a weak-
ness for favourites (in his case Bute) and inflated ideas on monarchy.
After a disastrous attempt at personal government he found in the
younger Pitt a prime minister in whom he could trust. His reign
embraced the close of the Seven Years War, the ceding of American
independence and the Napoleonic Wars: it was an era of vast industrial
and commercial growth and the golden age of British arts and letters.
His dull but respectable court and family life made him far more
popular than his dissolute sons; when his mental derangement was

first generally known in 1788 it evoked much sympathy and affection. The Prince of Wales became Regent in 1810.

PLATE 146. *Painting from the studio of A. Ramsay.* 58 × 42 in. No. 223.

JOHN GLYNN. 1722–1779.

Lawyer and politician; he acted as counsel for Wilkes. Serjeant-at-law, 1763; Recorder of London, 1772; M.P. for Middlesex, 1768–79.

PLATE 147. *Painting by Richard Houston.* 20¾ × 29¾ in. No. 1944.

JOHN WILKES. 1727–1797.

His contributions to *The North Briton* which he and Charles Churchill founded in 1762 led to his arrests and the parliamentary moves and counter-moves for which he was famous, and eventually to legal reforms, particularly the abolition of general warrants, freedom of election and freedom of speech. Despite his notorious private life he was honoured for his political integrity.

PLATE 147. *Painting by Richard Houston.* 20¾ × 29¾ in. No. 1944.

JOHN HORNE TOOKE. 1736–1812.

An ardent adherent of Wilkes until they squabbled violently in 1771. When an Enclosure Bill was introduced in 1774 his letter to *The Public Advertiser* reviling the Speaker led to the withdrawal of some 'obnoxious clauses' and started a bitter antagonism between him and Fox. His support of the American revolution led to his imprisonment in 1778. He published an important treatise on philology.

PLATE 147. *Painting by Richard Houston.* 20¾ × 29¾ in. No. 1944.

FREDERICK NORTH, 2ND EARL OF GUILFORD. 1732–1792.

As Prime Minister in 1770–82, often overborne by the King against his own judgment, he was responsible for the measures that brought about the loss of the American colonies. To this day his name is denigrated in America.

PLATE 148. *Painting from the studio of N. Dance.* 49 × 39 in. No. 3627.

SIR JOHN FIELDING. Died 1780.

Half-brother of Henry, the novelist, and blind from early youth, if not from birth. As a magistrate he was humane in his efforts for dealing with 'distressed' boys and 'deserted' girls. With his brother he founded the force of Bow Street Runners which foreshadowed the Criminal Investigation Department. In 1768 he published collected laws concerning offences in London.

PLATE 149. *Painting by Nathaniel Hone, 1762.* 49 × 39½ in. No. 3834.

SIR WILLIAM BLACKSTONE. 1723–1780.

First Vinerian Professor of English Law at Oxford, 1758–66; Judge of the Court of Common Pleas, 1770–80. His *Commentaries on the Laws of England* is still a standard work despite the attacks of Bentham and others.

PLATE 150. *Painting attributed to Reynolds.* 49 × 39¼ in. No. 388.

WARREN HASTINGS. 1732–1818.

First Governor-General of all British India, 1774–85. He carried forward Clive's work in building up alliances, and pursued a general policy of establishing British justice for the protection of Indians. Impeached on his return on a charge of peculation and extortion, his trial, which dragged on for seven years, ended in his acquittal but left him broken in health.

PLATE 151. *Painting by Tilly Kettle.* 27 × 22½ in. No. 81.

EDMUND BURKE. 1729–1797.

He held no high office of state, and his considerable influence in politics was due to the force and energy of his oratory and his writing. His speech 'On Conciliation with America' stands with the great classics of eloquence, his *Reflections on the Revolution in France* surpassed all other attacks, and his speech impeaching Warren Hastings lasted four days and evoked general wonder. Other themes on which his powers as writer and rhetorician had full play include the curbing of the power of the throne, the slave trade, the emancipation of Irish Catholics and Irish trade, and reform in Indian administration. He started the *Annual Register* in 1759, and for many years the greater part of it was written by him.

PLATE 152. *Painting from the studio of Reynolds.* 29¾ × 24¾ in. No. 655.

CHARLES WATSON-WENTWORTH, 2ND MARQUESS OF ROCKINGHAM. 1730–1782.

As Prime Minister in 1765 he repealed the odious Stamp Act imposed on the American colonies, and was dismissed in consequence. For the next sixteen years he led the Opposition. Some important reforms were achieved during his second term of office in 1782, though it lasted but four months.

PLATE 153. *Painting from the studio of Reynolds.* 27¼ × 22 in. No. 406.

WILLIAM PITT. 1759–1806.

Second son of William Pitt, Earl of Chatham. Prime Minister at twenty-four, he kept that office first for seventeen years, and for a further two in 1804–6. In the years of peace he applied the principles of freer trade advocated by Adam Smith, strengthening Britain for the war with France during which his resolution inspired the country, and his use of her financial resources, and his upkeep of a powerful navy brought eventual victory.

PLATE 154. *Painting by John Hoppner.* 55½ × 42½ in. No. 697.

CHARLES JAMES FOX. 1749–1806.

Whig politician. Throughout his career Fox was the champion of reform, and religious equality for Catholics and Dissenters. He also championed the rights of the American colonists and, regardless of popular odium, the French Revolution. His personal charm was phenomenal, and as a debater he ranked with the greatest. His persistent demand for Parliamentary reform prepared the way for the passing of the Bill in 1832.

PLATE 155. *Painting by Karl Anton Hickel.* 52 × 44½ in. No. 743.

ARTHUR PHILLIP. 1738–1814.

Admiral. In 1786 he was assigned the duty of forming the first settlement in Australia with six transports of convicts and troops. He landed at Botany Bay in 1788 and founded the colony at Sydney: after seeing it through great hardships, he returned to England in 1792.

PLATE 156. *Painting by Francis Wheatley, 1786.* 35½ × 27¼ in. No. 1462.

JAMES COOK. 1728–1779.

Given command of a scientific expedition, in 1768, he charted the coasts of New Zealand, the east coast of Australia and part of New Guinea, returning by the Cape of Good Hope in 1771. In 1772–5 he explored Pacific islands and Antarctic ice-fields, returning with his crew free from scurvy or fever. He discovered the Sandwich Islands in 1778; the following year he was killed by the natives of Hawaii.

PLATE 157. *Painting by John Webber.* 14½ × 11½ in. No. 26.

ADAM DUNCAN, 1st VISCOUNT DUNCAN. 1731–1804.

Admiral. After long and honourable service his most memorable achievements came in 1797 with his part in suppressing the mutinies at Spithead and the Nore; the blockade, with two ships, of 30,000 troops and the Dutch fleet in the Texel; and the bloody victory of Camperdown for which he was acclaimed his country's saviour.

PLATE 158. *Painting by John Hoppner.* 29½ × 24½ in. No. 1839.

RICHARD HOWE, 1st EARL HOWE. 1726–1799.

Admiral. His name is remembered with 'the Glorious First of June' of 1794, when, aged nearly seventy, he beat Villaret Joyeuse's fleet. His finest work, he reckoned, was the relief of Gibraltar in 1782. Nelson attributed the victory of the Nile largely to his improved system of signals. The old admiral's standing with the sailors enabled him to put an end to the Spithead mutiny in 1797.

PLATE 159. *Painting by Henry Singleton.* 22½ × 15½ in. No. 75.

HORATIO NELSON, VISCOUNT NELSON. 1758–1805.

Admiral. Starting with no advantage of patronage, he was a Post-captain before he was of age. His great opportunity arrived in 1798 when, after three months' pursuit, he came up with Napoleon's armada: he annihilated it in Aboukir Bay. In 1801, under Parker, he devised and carried through the Battle of the Baltic during which he misapplied his telescope. His crowning work was the great blockade of 1803–5 and the victory off Cape Trafalgar when he lost his life. Among his great qualities were his care and affection for his men and his genius for divining the movements of the enemy.

PLATE 160. *Painting by Lemuel Francis Abbott.* 29½ × 24½ in. No. 394.

EMMA, LADY HAMILTON. 1761?–1815.

Of humble parentage and great beauty, she was by 1781 under the protection of Charles Greville, then of his uncle, Sir William Hamilton, who married her at Naples in 1791. She became the confidante of the Queen of Naples and Nelson's 'own dear wife in my eyes and the face of Heaven'. She was Romney's favourite subject.

PLATE 161. *Painting by George Romney.* 29 × 23½ in. No. 294.

BENJAMIN FRANKLIN. 1706–1790.

American journalist and scientist who invented, among other things, the lightning conductor; his diplomatic career began with a mission to England in 1757; he stayed five years, receiving degrees at Oxford and Edinburgh. In 1764 he came over again to treat about improper taxation. He took a leading part in the Declaration of Independence, 4 July 1776, and then in enlisting French help for the Colonists, and was prominent among those who framed the American Constitution.

PLATE 162. *Painting after J. S. Duplessis.* 28 × 22½ in. No. 327.

GEORGE WASHINGTON. 1732–1799.

His finest quality as American Commander-in-Chief was his steadfast endurance in sustaining the struggle for independence despite the greatest difficulties. He was unanimously chosen to preside over the Federal Convention of 1787, from which emerged the Constitution of the United States, and in 1789 was elected first President. His Proclamation of American neutrality when England went to war with France in 1793 showed his wise statesmanship.

PLATE 163. *Painting by Gilbert Stuart.* 28¾ × 23¾ in. No. 2041.

SIR WILLIAM HAMILTON. 1730–1803.

Ambassador at Naples, 1764–1800. He helped in the excavations at Herculaneum and Pompeii, and collected Greek vases, now in the British Museum: his name is linked more particularly with the 'Portland Vase'.

PLATE 164. *Painting from the studio of Reynolds.* 100 × 69 in. No. 680.

JOSEPH PRIESTLEY. 1733–1804.

He discovered oxygen and was a pioneer of pneumatic chemistry. In 1767 he published *The History of Electricity*. As a Unitarian minister and leader of the movement for parliamentary reform he was the victim of a Birmingham 'Church and State' mob, wherefore he moved to Hackney; later he settled in America.

PLATE 165. *Chalk drawing after J. Sharples.* 8½ × 6¾ in. No. 175.

SIR WILLIAM HERSCHEL. 1738–1822.

Native of Hanover, he came to England in 1757 as a musician. Turning to astronomy, he discovered Uranus in 1781. He improved the telescope, perfected a polishing machine, and constructed a 40 ft. mirror. He discovered nebulae and made a study of their nature.

PLATE 166. *Painting by Lemuel Francis Abbott, 1785.* 29¼ × 24¼ in. No. 98.

JOHN SMEATON. 1724–1792.

He built the third Eddystone Lighthouse and several bridges, the Forth and Clyde canal, and a number of harbours, including those at St Ives and Ramsgate.

PLATE 167. *Painting by G. Romney after — Rhodes.* 29½ × 24½ in. No. 80.

SIR RICHARD ARKWRIGHT. 1732–1792.

Specialising in spinning machinery, he set up his spinning frame at Preston, and later, at Nottingham, his horse-powered spinning mill. At Cromford he started a water-powered factory, and in 1775 patented inventions for combining in one machine the whole process of yarn manufacture. In 1790 he introduced the Boulton and Watt steam-engine into his Nottingham mill.

PLATE 168. *Painting by Joseph Wright.* 29½ × 24½ in. No. 136.

JOHN HUNTER. 1728–1793.

Anatomist and surgeon; widely regarded as the founder of scientific surgery. His museum was bought by the Government in 1799 for £15,000 and installed in the Royal College of Surgeons: a part of it was destroyed by enemy action in 1941.

PLATE 169. *Painting by J. Jackson after Reynolds.* 55½ × 43¼ in. No. 77.

JAMES WATT. 1736–1819.

From harbour surveying he turned his attention to the steam-engine and made important improvements, such as the separate condenser, the air-pump and double-stroke engine. He became partner of Boulton at Soho, Birmingham; they marketed the first practical cylindrical steam-engines which revolutionised world industry, replacing horse-and water-power.

PLATE 170. *Painting by Carl Fredrik von Breda, 1792.* 49½ × 39½ in. No. 186A.

JOHN HOWARD. 1726?–1790.

Thanks to him two prison reform acts were passed in England in 1774, enforcing prison cleanliness, and fixing jailers' pay in order to remedy the extortion practised on prisoners. He travelled some 50,000 miles visiting the disease-infected prisons of Europe: in 1777 he published *The State of Prisons...*, and in 1780 *An Account of the Principal Lazarettos in Europe.*

PLATE 171. *Painting by Mather Brown.* 27¾ × 23 in. No. 97.

THOMAS CLARKSON. 1760–1846.

Philanthropist. A leader of the anti-slavery agitation and indefatigable in proselytising and in collecting evidence. He shared with Wilberforce the honour of securing the abolition of the trade in 1807, and of West Indian slavery in 1833. He founded seamen's homes and institutions.

PLATE 172. *Painting by Carl Fredrik von Breda, 1789.* 35 × 27½ in. No. 235.

THOMAS GRAY. 1716–1771.

Poet and medieval scholar. His *Elegy written in a Country Churchyard*, on which he worked for six years, is one of the finest and best-known poems of that century. The earlier *Ode on a Distant Prospect of Eton* is next in popular affection, though the later Pindaric odes, *The Bard* and *Progress of Poesy* are in some opinions his greatest work. Later he steeped himself in Norse and Welsh poetry. He is one of our best letter-writers.

PLATE 173. *Painting by John Giles Eccardt, 1748.* 15½ × 12¼ in. No. 989.

HORACE WALPOLE, 4TH EARL OF ORFORD. 1717–1797.

The *Anecdotes of Painting*, arranged and amplified from Vertue's note-books, which is the basis of our knowledge of artists working in England before the early eighteenth century, is one of the most lastingly important of his many writings. His novel, *The Castle of Otranto*, published in 1764, was almost the first literary manifestation of the Gothic revival. For many years his interests centred in Strawberry Hill, his 'little Gothic castle' at Twickenham, which he enlarged, adorned and filled to overflowing with *objets d'art et virtu*. For wit, often waspish, and range of subjects his *Letters* are perhaps the finest in the language, and his *Memoirs* sharply illumine the history of his time. Too often his very considerable parts were dissipated in the pursuit of social tittle-tattle and artistic knick-knackery.

PLATE 174. *Painting by John Giles Eccardt, 1754.* 15½ × 12½ in. No. 988.

ROBERT RAIKES. 1735–1811.

In 1780 he opened a Sunday school in Gloucester and made widely known the principle of cheap schooling. He lived to see such schools spread over England.

PLATE 175. *Paste medallion by William Tassie.* 3 × 2¼ in. No. 2548.

ADAM SMITH. 1723–1790.

Scottish political economist, author of *Enquiry into the Nature and Causes of the Wealth of Nations* (1776), which has had a profound influence on political thought and practice: his principles were promptly applied by his disciples, Pitt the younger and Canning. He was the friend of Hume, Blair and Robertson at home, and abroad of Turgot, Necker and Voltaire.

PLATE 176. *Paste medallion by James Tassie, 1787.* 3½ × 2½ in. No. 3237.

JOSIAH WEDGWOOD. 1730–1795.

From a provincial craft he brought English pottery to a fine art, applying his knowledge of classic art to the forms and decoration of his wares, and perfecting their fabric. Flaxman, when a youth of twenty, was one of the artists he trained and employed. In 1858 Gladstone prophesied that when British manufactures became as famous for their taste as for their cheapness it would be due to Wedgwood.

PLATE 177. *Wedgwood-ware medallion by William Hackwood, 1779.* 5 × 4 in. No. 1948.

EDWARD GIBBON. 1737–1794.

Intoxicated by his first experience of Rome in 1764, he conceived the idea of his *Decline and Fall of the Roman Empire*. He devoted years to minute research and the first volume appeared in 1776, the last two in 1788. Gibbon's art, or style, is famous: rhythmic and sonorous: 'The sound is always musical, and the pomp has true majesty'; it 'gave distinction to historical writing', just as his concentration on the idea of decline and fall 'gave meaning to historical thinking'.

PLATE 178. *Painting by Henry Walton.* 9 × 6½ in. No. 1443.

ROBERT BURNS. 1759–1796.

Scottish farmer—'a heaven-taught plowman'—and a great poet. He is revered and quoted by Britons everywhere, for all he wrote largely in the vernacular, and is well-nigh worshipped in Scotland where the anniversary of his birth is a great national festival celebrated with a precise ritual. Writing recently, a countryman said 'Down the years Burns has bound us Scots in a great and indivisible brotherhood which puzzles other nations and sometimes ourselves.' As a writer of verse for songs he is unsurpassed and we owe him many of those we know best, such as *My Love is like a Red Red Rose* and *Auld Lang Syne*.

PLATE 179. *Painting by Alexander Nasmyth.* 12½ × 9½ in. No. 46.

WILLIAM COWPER. 1731–1800.
Poet and letter-writer. His most familiar works are the noble *Toll for the Brave, John Gilpin's Ride* and a number of hymns. *The Task*, in blank verse, was his most ambitious piece; its protest against Pope's 'mere mechanic art' greatly impressed his contemporaries. His letters, describing his country life, and ranging over many years, are as delightful in their matter as in their easy, limpid manner.

PLATE 180. *Painting by Lemuel Francis Abbott, 1792.* 50 × 40 in. No. 2783.

LAURENCE STERNE. 1713–1768.
A country parson, and the author of *Tristram Shandy* and *A Sentimental Journey*. His coarseness of language and of innuendo was generally censured; nevertheless, both these works won immediate success and have kept their place as masterpieces of comedy. They depend not at all on organised plot, and both humour and characterisation spring largely from his perception of what passes irrationally in man's mind. In this he anticipates the 'interior monologue' of some twentieth-century novelists.

PLATE 181. *Painting by an unknown artist.* 16¾ × 13½ in. No. 2022.

ROBERT ADAM. 1728–1792.
Architect. Friend of Clérisseau and Piranesi, student in Italy and Dalmatia, he was a great eclectic and innovator, fusing many influences into a style completely his own and revolutionising English architecture and furnishing. His outstanding work as an interior architect can still be studied at such houses as Syon, Kenwood, Osterley and Stowe, but the lovely piece of London street architecture, The Adelphi, designed and built by him and his brothers between 1768 and 1771 was destroyed in the twentieth century—not by enemy action.

PLATE 182. *Painting by an unknown artist.* 50 × 40 in. No. 2953.

RICHARD WILSON. 1713?–1782.
Early in life he painted some portraits, but after visiting Italy, 1749–56, devoted himself to landscapes. The influence of Claude particularly, assimilated and transmuted into English lyrical poetry, is clearly seen in his paintings. Through him, more than any other, the classic Italian expression of landscape pervaded England, and though during his lifetime he suffered neglect, artists as widely different as Crome and Turner were greatly in his debt.

PLATE 183. *Painting after A. R. Mengs.* 29½ × 24½ in. No. 1803.

THOMAS GAINSBOROUGH. 1727–1788.

He and Reynolds were the greatest English portrait painters. Where Reynolds was the more scholarly, more inventive, and more able designer, Gainsborough, with the sweeping, rhythmic play of his brush, was the finer painter and the better colourist. In characterisation Reynolds, on the whole, was more robust and actual, Gainsborough more nervously perceptive. Unlike Reynolds he also painted landscapes of a rare and lyric loveliness.

PLATE 184. *Painting by John Zoffany.* $7\frac{1}{2} \times 6\frac{1}{2}$ in. No. 3913.

SIR JOSHUA REYNOLDS. 1723–1792.

One of the greatest, most respected and successful of English portrait painters. He was largely responsible for founding the Royal Academy in 1768 when he became President and delivered the first of his Discourses. In 1764 he founded 'The Club' in order to 'give Dr Johnson unlimited opportunities for talking'.

PLATE 185. *Painting by himself.* $25 \times 29\frac{1}{4}$ in. No. 41.

DR SAMUEL JOHNSON. 1709–1784.

Author of the *Dictionary of the English Language* which he completed single handed between 1747 and 1755, and of essays, biographies, plays and poetry. He was a man of sombre piety, and vast erudition, a great master of resounding English prose and a great, if somewhat overbearing, talker whose particular delight was to deflate his interlocutors by a trenchant statement of the matter of fact.

PLATE 186. *Painting by Sir Joshua Reynolds, 1756.* 49×39 in. No. 1597.

CHARLES BURNEY. 1726–1814.

Organist, conductor and teacher of music; the author of a number of miscellaneous literary and musical compositions and of a *History of Music* published in four volumes between 1776 and 1789. He was a popular figure in polite society and a member of 'The Club': he was also the father of Fanny Burney and of the classical scholar, Dr Charles Burney.

PLATE 187. *Painting by Sir Joshua Reynolds, 1781.* $29\frac{1}{2} \times 24$ in. No. 3884.

FRANCES D'ARBLAY (NÉE BURNEY). 1752–1840.

Daughter of Dr Burney: author of *Evelina*, *Cecilia* and other novels. As a young authoress she was made much of by Mrs Thrale, Dr Johnson and their circle. From 1786 to 1790 she was Second Keeper of the Queen's Robes. In 1793 she married General D'Arblay, a French refugee. Her diaries describing in detail her life at court and later in France were published after her death.

PLATE 188. *Painting by Edward Francis Burney.* 30 × 25 in. No. 2634.

OLIVER GOLDSMITH. 1728–1774.

Author of the novel, *The Vicar of Wakefield,* the play, *She Stoops to Conquer,* and the poem, *The Deserted Village.* He led a restless life, and though a member of 'The Club' and much loved by Johnson and other close friends, was over-anxious to shine and at his worst in society; hence Garrick's saying '...he wrote like an angel but talked like poor Poll'.

PLATE 189. *Painting from the studio of Reynolds.* 29 × 24½ in. No. 130.

JAMES BOSWELL. 1740–1795.

Scottish lawyer and country gentleman with a passion for society and celebrities, and an incomparable gift for vivid reporting. He attached himself to Dr Johnson and, in 1791, published a *Life* of him which is one of the greatest masterpieces of biography. His very revealing journals show him bumptious, eager, affable, thick-skinned, pretty nearly shameless and possessed of quite astonishing resilience.

PLATE 190. *Painting by Sir Joshua Reynolds, 1786.* 28½ × 23¾ in. No. 1675.

JOSEPH WRIGHT OF DERBY. 1734–1797.

He painted portraits, landscapes and lamplight *genre,* excelling in the last, wherefore he has been called the English Honthorst.

PLATE 191. *Painting by himself.* 28½ × 23¾ in. No. 29.

JOHN ZOFFANY. 1734/5–1810.

Painter of German birth and a roving disposition. As a youth he spent twelve years in Italy. He first exhibited in London, in 1762, Garrick in a scene from *The Farmer's Return:* by 1769 when he was elected a Royal Academician he was enjoying royal patronage. He paid a second visit of six years to Italy, and after another four years in London set off for India: the last twenty years of his life were spent in London. He was the ablest of the painters of theatrical scenes and 'conversation pieces' and his landscape backgrounds are admirable.

PLATE 192. *Painting by himself, 1761.* 20¾ × 16¼ in. No. 399.

JOHN OPIE. 1761–1807.
Painter. Son of a west-country carpenter, and supposed to have been self-taught, he was produced in London with some *éclat* about 1782 by 'Peter Pindar' and well advertised as 'The Cornish Wonder'. Although he became popular as a portrait painter, his genius was ill-suited to the sophistication of society sitters and he was at his best with his more direct and natural subjects. His 'history' paintings also were much praised.
PLATE 193. *Painting by himself, 1785.* 29¼ × 24½ in. No. 47.

JAMES NORTHCOTE. 1746–1831.
He lived with Reynolds from 1771 to 1775 as pupil and assistant, and then studied in Rome. He had a large practice as portrait painter and did a great many *genre* and 'history' paintings of which perhaps the best known is 'The Murder of the Princes in the Tower' now at Petworth. He wrote the life of Sir Joshua Reynolds and of Titian.
PLATE 194. *Painting by himself, 1784.* 29 × 24 in. No. 3253.

GEORGE ROMNEY. 1734–1802.
Portrait painter; the runner-up of Gainsborough and Reynolds. Lacking their mastery of characterisation, he got by very comfortably on his ability to give an air of consequence to all his sitters. His artistic integrity was not proof against extreme prettiness as may be seen from his many portraits—perhaps forty or fifty—of Emma Hamilton.
PLATE 195. *Painting by himself, 1782.* 49½ × 39 in. No. 959.

NATHANIEL HONE. 1718–1784.
Founder member of the Royal Academy, exhibiting there until his death. He worked in oils, enamel and mezzotint.
PLATE 196. *Painting by himself.* 29½ × 24 in. No. 177.

ALLAN RAMSAY. 1713–1784.
Portrait painter of Scottish birth, the forerunner of Gainsborough and of Reynolds whom he anticipated in the introduction into British portraiture of something of the Italian grand manner. At his best he showed a rare delicacy and distinction and a lively invention in design.
PLATE 197. *Painting by himself.* 23½ × 18 in. No. 3311.

DAVID GARRICK. 1717–1779.
The actor who, according to Burke, 'raised the character of his profession to the rank of a liberal art'. He was highly successful as

patentee and manager of Drury Lane; he wrote or adapted a number of plays and composed a great many prologues and epilogues for his productions. So popular was he, on and off the stage, that at his funeral the carriages reached from Westminster Abbey to the Strand and the pall-bearers included the Duke of Devonshire, Lords Camden, Ossory, Spencer and Palmerston, and Fox, Burke and Dr Johnson who said his death '...eclipsed the gaiety of nations'.

PLATE 198. *Painting by Robert Edge Pine.* 35 × 28 in. No. 82.

JOHN PHILIP KEMBLE. 1757–1823.

Actor, dramatist and patentee; brother of Sarah Siddons. His first London success was as Hamlet at Drury Lane in 1783: in 1788 he became Sheridan's manager, and in 1802 manager of Covent Garden, taking his sister with him. Hazlitt regarded him as the best actor of his time.

PLATE 199. *Painting by Gilbert Stuart.* 29½ × 24½ in. No. 49.

RICHARD BRINSLEY SHERIDAN. 1751–1816.

Playwright, politician, theatrical manager and orator. His comedies— *The Rivals* and *The School for Scandal*, with their famous characters Mrs Malaprop, Bob Acres, Sir Lucius O'Trigger, Lady Teazle, and the Surfaces—stand today with the most brilliant in the language. As orator impeaching Warren Hastings, he shared the honours with Burke. His wife was the beautiful Elizabeth Linley.

PLATE 200. *Painting by John Russell, 1788.* 23½ × 17½ in. No. 651.

THOMAS AUGUSTINE ARNE. 1710–1778.

His early passion and talent for music having overcome formidable parental opposition he devoted his life to composing songs, operas and incidental music, and to teaching. His wife, Cecilia Arne, and his sister, Mrs Cibber, sang in many of his productions. His output was enormous: best known today are the music for *Comus*, the settings of Shakespeare songs such as *Where the Bee Sucks*, and *Rule Britannia*.

PLATE 201. *Coloured etching after Bartolozzi.* 11 × 8¾ in. No. 1130.

MARY ('PERDITA') ROBINSON (née DARBY). 1758–1800.

Actress and mistress of the Prince of Wales (later George IV) whom she attracted when playing Perdita in *The Winter's Tale*. Gainsborough's portraits of her are at Windsor and in the Wallace Collection.

PLATE 202. *Drawing by George Dance.* 10¼ × 8¼ in. No. 1254.

SARAH SIDDONS (née Kemble). 1755-1831.

At first, playing with Garrick at Drury Lane in 1775-6 she was a failure; touring in the provinces with Tate Wilkinson and Palmer, a brilliant success. Later with Garrick at Drury Lane, and with her brother John Philip Kemble at Covent Garden she established her reputation as England's greatest tragedienne.

PLATE 203. *Drawing by John Donnman, 1787.* 8 × 6¾ in. No. 2651.

ELIZABETH STANLEY, COUNTESS OF DERBY (née Farren). 1759?-1829.

Actress; born in Cork, she succeeded Mrs Abington as the leading comedienne. Lord Derby (with whom her name was connected from 1791) married her in 1797. Femininely, Mrs Thrale 'believed' that Miss Farren 'is now all that Man desires in Woman', and Hazlitt praised her 'fine-lady airs and graces'.

PLATE 204. *Drawing by John Downman, 1787.* 8 × 6¾ in. No. 2652.

FREDERIC, DUKE OF YORK AND ALBANY. 1763-1827.

Second son of George III. As a young man he was sent to learn soldiering in Germany, and in 1793/4, at the insistence of the King, was given command of the forces in Flanders. He was a competent, by no means brilliant general, but was fighting against heavy odds with badly trained and equipped troops, three other generals to 'help' him in the field and Dundas issuing orders from the War Office. All the odium for the ill-success of the campaign, however, and for one at Helder in 1799, fell on him. He had no head for politics, and he was involved in deplorable scandals, but his work as Commander-in-Chief was of the greatest importance. He founded the Royal Military College at Woolwich for training officers, improved conditions and training for the men, and built up an efficient army which Wellington was able to use when the time came.

PLATE 205. *Painting by Sir David Wilkie, 1823.* 23¼ × 20½ in. No. 2936.

ERNEST AUGUSTUS, DUKE OF CUMBERLAND AND KING OF HANOVER. 1771-1851.

Fifth son of George III. Unlike his brothers he was thin, taciturn, and a considerable force in politics as a High Tory. He was contemptuous of public opinion and in the popular estimation capable of any un-scrupulous and scandalous iniquity. He was a fierce and fearless soldier, an officer in both the British and the Hanoverian army, and a harsh disciplinarian. On the death without male issue of his brother, William IV, he became King of Hanover where it appears that he ruled well and was liked and respected.

PLATE 206. *Painting by George Dawe.* 35¼ × 27½ in. No. 3309.

KING GEORGE IV. 1762–1830.
Eldest son of George III; Prince Regent from 1811 and King from 1820. During the Regency England won some of her proudest victories by sea and land, and produced some of her finest works of art and literature. The Prince was a fitting, slightly *outré*, symbol of the period. Unstable and impolitic, perhaps; selfish and self-indulgent, certainly; extravagant beyond comparison in an age of extravagance; but lively, cultured, with immense charm and perfect manners. Let those who will deride his taste as typified by the Pavilion at Brighton, but let them also remember that he had a fine knowledge and appreciation of old master paintings, gave encouragement to John Nash and greatly admired the novels of Miss Austen.

PLATE 207. *Painting by Sir Thomas Lawrence.* 27 × 20½ in. No. 123.

PRINCESS CHARLOTTE AUGUSTA OF WALES. 1796–1817.
Daughter of George IV. As a child she was brought up largely by her grandmother, Queen Charlotte, and grew to be a gay, high spirited and popular young woman. In 1813 she became engaged to William, Prince of Orange, but she broke off the engagement, and in 1816 married Prince Leopold of Saxe-Coburg. She died in childbirth, greatly mourned.

PLATE 208. *Painting by George Dawe.* 55 × 42½ in. No. 51.

CAROLINE OF BRUNSWICK. 1768–1821.
Daughter of Charles, Duke of Brunswick-Wolfenbüttel, and niece of George III. She was chosen as the wife of the Prince of Wales, later George IV, and though they had never met, came to England in 1795 and was married to him. It was a singularly unsuitable match, and after a year they separated. After 1813 she lived abroad for some years, and the scandals created by her unseemly behaviour culminated in his attempt to divorce her in 1820. The case was abandoned for reasons of policy, not for lack of evidence, and though she lived thereafter in England she was never officially recognised as Queen.

PLATE 209. *Painting by Sir Thomas Lawrence.* 55¼ × 44 in. No. 244.

ARTHUR WELLESLEY, 1st DUKE OF WELLINGTON. 1769–1852.

His first resounding victory was at Assaye in India in 1803: he won the long Peninsular War in 1814 and beat Napoleon at Waterloo in 1815. His prowess as a military commander made him, even during his lifetime and not only in England, a legendary hero—'the Iron Duke'. Later he devoted himself and the full weight of his immense prestige to politics and was Prime Minister in 1828–30 and in 1834. He was the trusted friend and adviser of Queen Victoria and Prince Albert and godfather to their third son: in 1850 the Queen said 'How powerful and how clear the mind of this wonderful man is, and how honest and how loyal and kind he is to us both.'

PLATE 210. *Painting by John Jackson.* 49½ × 39½ in. No. 1614.

SIR JOHN MOORE. 1761–1809.

Hero of Corunna. His advance against Napoleon's army in 1808 saved the Peninsula; heavily outnumbered, he extricated his army through the mountains and reached Corunna where Soult was waiting to destroy it while embarking. Moore was killed in his brilliantly successful covering action. His burial inspired Charles Wolfe's famous dirge.

PLATE 211. *Painting by Sir Thomas Lawrence.* 29½ × 24½ in. No. 1128.

SIR GRAHAM MOORE. 1764–1843.

Admiral. He captured four treasure ships off the Spanish coast in 1803, and served in the Walcheren expedition in 1809. In 1820 he was Commander-in-Chief in the Mediterranean.

PLATE 212. *Painting by Sir Thomas Lawrence.* 29½ × 25 in. No. 1129.

GEORGE CANNING. 1770–1827.

During his first term as Foreign Secretary, in 1807–8, Napoleon's northern confederacy was finally disabled by the capture of the Danish fleet. During his second term, from 1822 to 1827, he showed himself resolutely against armed intervention in foreign affairs by England or other powers, and his recognition of the independence of the Spanish American colonies was prompted by French interference in Spain. He was determined to use every means short of going to war to bring about the freedom of Greece from Turkey. By 1827, when he succeeded Lord Liverpool, he was already ailing and he was Prime Minister for only a few troubled months.

PLATE 213. *Detail from a painting by Sir Thomas Lawrence.* No. 1832.

ROBERT BANKS JENKINSON, 2ND EARL OF LIVERPOOL. 1770–1828.

Tory statesman. As Prime Minister, 1812–27, he strongly supported Wellington in the Peninsular War, and he showed great skill in managing a brilliant team which included Castlereagh, Huskisson, Canning and Palmerston.

PLATE 214. *Detail from a painting by Sir Thomas Lawrence.* No. 1804.

ROBERT STEWART, 2ND MARQUESS OF LONDONDERRY (LORD CASTLEREAGH). 1769–1822.

As Foreign Secretary in 1813–15 he negotiated in Paris and Vienna to compass the fall of Napoleon, to preserve the Concert of Europe, to restrain the avarice of the Czar and curb Prussian expansion. His statesmanship in dealing with the United States after the war of 1812 secured Canada's frontier. In the post-war depression and disillusion he was blamed for the repressive policy of his colleagues, and his mind became unhinged; his suicide was brutally acclaimed by the mob. He was a man of scrupulous integrity, courage and tenacity.

PLATE 215. *Painting by Sir Thomas Lawrence.* 29¼ × 24¼ in. No. 891.

WILLIAM HUSKISSON. 1770–1830.

Statesman and financial expert; in economics the disciple of Adam Smith and Pitt: an adherent of Canning. As President of the Board of Trade (1823–7) he pioneered in Free Trade and went some way towards abolishing the Navigation Acts. He was killed by an engine at the opening of the Manchester and Liverpool railway.

PLATE 216. *Painting by Richard Rothwell.* 35¼ × 27¼ in. No. 21.

SIR THOMAS STAMFORD BINGLEY RAFFLES. 1781–1826.

Lieutenant-Governor of Java from its capture in 1811 till it was restored to the Dutch in 1815; thereafter Governor of Bencoolen. His great energy and ability as administrator and his zeal for the well-being of the natives made him one of the greatest and best servants of the Empire. His *History of Java* (1817) embodies his great scientific and philological knowledge of East India. In 1819 he persuaded the East India Company to buy the island of Singapore. After retiring in 1824 and settling in England he founded the Zoological Society and was the first President.

PLATE 217. *Painting by George Francis Joseph, 1817.* 55 × 43 in. No. 84.

JEREMY BENTHAM. 1748-1832.

Legal philosopher and law reformer; father of 'utilitarian' radicalism. From Priestley he adopted the doctrine of 'the greatest happiness of the greatest number', and as a reformer he was concerned less with morality than with human betterment. He advocated universal suffrage and annual parliaments.

PLATE 218. *Painting by Henry William Pickersgill, 1829.* 80½ × 54½ in. No. 413.

WILLIAM WILBERFORCE. 1759-1833.

The leader of the anti-slavery campaign in parliament. After several set-backs the bill abolishing the slave trade was passed in 1807, and the emancipation bill in 1833. Himself an Evangelical by conversion, a philanthropist, and a man of persuasive charm and integrity, he had an extraordinary influence in society and politics, and exerted it for parliamentary reform and religious tolerance.

PLATE 219. *Painting by Sir Thomas Lawrence, 1828.* 38 × 43 in. No. 3.

WILLIAM BLAKE. 1757-1827.

Visionary poet, painter and engraver. In power of conception and imagination Blake stands with the greatest artists, graphic and poetic. His range, from the touching simplicity of innocence to fierce, if obscure, splendour, is unexampled. The confluence in him of mystic poet and artist effected the rare quality of his expression.

PLATE 220. *Painting by Thomas Phillips, 1807.* 35½ × 27¼ in. No. 212.

MARY GODWIN (NÉE WOLLSTONECRAFT). 1759-1797.

Authoress and feminist. Her *Vindication of the Rights of Women* (1792) advocates equality of education for the sexes and state-controlled co-education. By Gilbert Imlay she had a daughter, Fanny, and by William Godwin, whom she married in 1797, another Mary, who became Shelley's second wife. Blake illustrated her *Original Stories*.

PLATE 221. *Painting by John Opie.* 29½ × 24½ in. No. 1237.

WILLIAM WORDSWORTH. 1770-1850.

One of the earliest of the 'Romantic' poets. His constant theme was nature, sublime and awful or serene and reassuring, in relation to his own soul; particularly he exalted in the English lake country. No other major poet ever wrote so much bad verse. When he practised his theory that the language of poetry should be identical with that of real life his banality and triviality justly met with parody and ridicule: when at his best he could produce such masterpieces as *Tintern Abbey*, the *Ode on Intimations of Immortality*, or the sonnet, *Upon Westminster Bridge*. His poetry had little success when first published and recognition came very slowly, but eventually he won the respect due to 'the first of living poets' and on the death of Southey in 1843 it seemed a matter of course that he should be chosen poet laureate.

PLATE 222. *Drawing by Robert Hancock, 1798.* $6\frac{1}{2} \times 5\frac{1}{2}$ in. No. 450.

CHARLES LAMB. 1775–1834.

Poet, essayist and critic. Most widely remembered for his *Tales from Shakespeare*, written with his sister Mary, and for the first and last *Essays of Elia* (1820–33). With Mary he also wrote *Mrs Leicester's School* and *Poems for Children*, delightful in their pathos and humour, which, antiphonally, give the 'Elia' essays their peculiar charm. His best-known poem is the *Old Familiar Faces*.

PLATE 223. *Drawing by Robert Hancock, 1798.* $6\frac{3}{4} \times 5\frac{3}{4}$ in. No. 449.

SAMUEL TAYLOR COLERIDGE. 1772–1834.

Poet, philosopher, critic and metaphysician. His three best poems, *The Ancient Mariner*, the first part of *Christabel*, and *Kubla Khan*, which has been said to 'stand alone for melody in English poetry', were composed between November 1797 and May 1798. His last great poem is *Dejection* (1802). Later he was occupied mainly with literary criticism and philosophy. Both in his writings and conversation he exerted wide influence.

PLATE 224. *Drawing by Robert Hancock, 1796.* $6\frac{1}{2} \times 5\frac{1}{2}$ in. No. 452.

ROBERT SOUTHEY. 1774–1843.

Author and poet laureate. His *Life of Nelson* (1813) is still regarded as a masterpiece of prose; as poet he is remembered by the *Holly Tree*, *Blenheim* and *The Inchcape Rock*. That nursery classic, *The Three Bears*, comes in his miscellany, *The Doctor* (1834–47).

PLATE 225. *Drawing by Robert Hancock, 1796.* $6\frac{3}{4} \times 5\frac{3}{4}$ in. No. 451.

SIR WALTER SCOTT, BART. 1771–1832.

His ebullient gift for story telling, his familiarity from childhood with Scottish and ancestral history and legend, his antiquarian tastes, his knowledge of the Scottish countryside and its ballads and stories, are all ingredients which give a rich and exciting flavour to his writing. His first great success was *The Lay of the Last Minstrel* published in

1805. *Waverley*, begun as early as 1805, and finished in 1814, was so popular that he wrote novels thereafter at the rate of nearly one a year. He made enormous sums of money by his writing and spent even more, largely on buying, rebuilding, enlarging, embellishing and fillng with curios his country house at Abbottsford.

PLATE 226. *Painting by Sir Edwin Henry Landseer, 1824.* $11\frac{1}{2} \times 9\frac{1}{2}$ in. No. 391.

GEORGE GORDON BYRON, 6TH BARON BYRON. 1788–1824.

Despite his erratic temperament, his exhibitionism and excesses he was a great poet. He 'awoke and found himself famous' when cantos I and II of *Childe Harold's Pilgrimage* appeared. *Don Juan* came out between 1819 and 1824: 'All life is here in its various phases of love and joy, suffering and hate and fear.' *Prometheus*, too, is ranked with his finest utterances. He travelled frequently and lived much abroad, and, intent on helping Greece in her fight for freedom from Turkish rule, he went to Missolonghi where he died of fever.

PLATE 227. *Painting by Thomas Phillips.* $29\frac{1}{2} \times 24\frac{1}{2}$ in. No. 142.

JOHN KEATS. 1795–1821.

His early poetry, which included the sonnet *On first Looking into Chapman's Homer*, though rudely slated by some of the critics and ignored by the public, was of a quality to impress his more perceptive literary friends, but no sooner had he gained true mastery of his craft than he was gripped by mortal illness. In the space of only some twenty short and troubled months, from the spring of 1818 when he wrote *Isabella and the Pot of Basil*, he wrote those poems, including *The Eve of St Agnes, La Belle Dame Sans Merci, Lamia*, and the odes *On a Grecian Urn, To a Nightingale* and *To Autumn*, which are of such magic and sad, haunting loveliness, and ensure his place in 'the abode where the Eternal are'.

PLATE 228. *Miniature by Joseph Severn, 1819.* $4\frac{1}{4} \times 3\frac{1}{8}$ in. No. 1605.

PERCY BYSSHE SHELLEY. 1792–1822.

His prose essay, *A Defence of Poetry*, one of the most inspired affirmations of the value of the arts, and his greatest poems, including *Prometheus Unbound, The Cenci, Epipsychidion*, the *Ode to the West Wind, To a Skylark* and the elegy on Keats, *Adonais*, were written during the last four or five years of his short and sadly complicated existence. Unworldly, elusive—'tameless, and swift, and proud'—he constantly, as he put it, 'made the error of seeking in a mortal image the likeness of what is, perhaps, eternal'. Yet in his own image, as it survives, he seems the very personification of the poetic spirit.

PLATE 229. *Painting by Amelia Curran, 1819.* 23½ × 18¾ in. No. 1234.

JOHN SELL COTMAN. 1782–1842.

Painter, of Norwich. One of the greatest stylists of landscape, with an understanding and expression of the essential dignity of nature. His austere selection and simplification, that yet interpret the quality of nature, place him apart.

PLATE 230. *Water-colour by Horace Beevor Love, 1830.* 10½ × 8 in. No. 1372.

JOHN CROME. 1768–1821.

Painter; father of the Norwich School. In the best sense a rustic master, self-trained on traditional lines but untainted by current fashions. In his most individual work he anticipated Constable in impressionism.

PLATE 231. *Water-colour by Denis Brownell Murphy.* 7¼ × 6 in. No. 2061.

JOHN CONSTABLE. 1776–1837.

Painter. Mainly self-taught, he did not exhibit till he was twenty-six. His career was a struggle between his natural perception of nature's breadth, light and movement and the 'finish' that was expected of him. His natural bent won with unsurpassed renderings of open air, fleeting light and shade, and the very life of wind-driven clouds. He freed landscape painting from convention and laid the lines of its future development.

PLATE 232. *Water-colour by himself.* 10 × 8 in. No. 901.

WILLIAM HAZLITT. 1778–1830.

Critic, essayist and journalist. His pithy commonsense, brisk style and shrewd taste, not to mention his positive self-assurance and descriptive aptness, make his essays not only entertaining but stimulating. His criticism of art and of literature is often most perceptive and his *Conversations of James Northcote* is a mine of curious information. Many critics have held that *The Spirit of the Age* is his best book.

PLATE 233. *Drawing by William Bewick.* 22¾ × 14¾ in. No. 2697.

JOHN NASH. 1752–1835.

Regency architect and town-planner. His great achievement was the development of Regent's Park, linking it with Carlton House by his Royal Mile (Regent Street) and the addition of Carlton House Terrace. His wayward genius made that part of London one of the most charming and impressive places. Later generations have seen to it that barely anything of his Regent Street survives, save in Shotter Boys's lithographs.

PLATE 234. *Wax medallion by Joseph Anton Couriguer.* $3\frac{3}{4}$ in. diameter. No. 2778.

JANE AUSTEN. 1775–1817.

With 'genius, wit and taste to recommend them' her novels stand alone, acknowledged as the most perfect works of their kind. Among her many gifts she had, as Sir Walter Scott put it, 'the exquisite touch which renders ordinary common-place things and characters interesting from the truth of the description and the sentiment'. *Sense and Sensibility* was published in 1811, *Pride and Prejudice* in 1813, *Mansfield Park* in 1814, *Emma*, dedicated by his request to the Prince Regent, in 1816, and *Northanger Abbey* and *Persuasion* posthumously in 1818.

PLATE 235. *Water-colour by Cassandra Elizabeth Austen.* $4\frac{1}{2} \times 3\frac{1}{2}$ in. No. 3630.

JOSEPH MALLORD WILLIAM TURNER. 1775–1851.

Perhaps the most significant painter since Rembrandt. His perception of nature was revolutionary, and in landscape painting he bridged the gap between Constable and the Impressionists of the nineteenth century. His achievement has not been challenged by any later painter.

PLATE 236. *Drawing by Charles Martin.* $13\frac{3}{4} \times 9\frac{1}{2}$ in. No. 1483.

KING WILLIAM IV. 1765–1837.

The third son of George III, and known as the Duke of Clarence until he succeeded his brother, George IV. From an early age he served in the Navy—not without causing trouble from time to time —and in 1807/8 was Lord High Admiral. For more than twenty years he lived in contented domesticity with the actress, Mrs Jordan, but in 1818 after the death of Princess Charlotte, heir to the throne, he married Princess Adelaide. He affected the bluff manners of a sailor and had an eccentric disregard for etiquette; he was choleric and had fierce likes and dislikes, but behind the bluster he had perhaps more wisdom than was generally allowed. His support of the Whigs—albeit reluctant—enabled them to pass the great Parliamentary Reform Bill of 1832.

PLATE 237. *Painting by Sir Martin Archer Shee.* 87 × 59 in. No. 2199.

ADELAIDE OF SAXE-MEININGEN. 1792–1849.

Eldest daughter of George, Duke of Saxe-Meiningen. In 1818 she married the Duke of Clarence, later William IV: no child of the marriage survived. For a time, during the reform agitation, she became very unpopular, but eventually her goodness and her charitable generosity won general respect and admiration. Adelaide, the capital of South Australia, first settled in 1836, was named after her.

PLATE 238. *Painting by Sir William Beechy.* 34¼ × 28½ in. No. 1533.

MARIA LOUISA VICTORIA, DUCHESS OF KENT. 1786–1861.

The daughter of Francis Frederick Anthony, Duke of Saxe-Coburg-Saalfeld. In 1818 she married, as her second husband, Edward, Duke of Kent, and their only child, Alexandrina Victoria, was born the following year. For the next eighteen years she devoted herself entirely to the care and education of the future Queen.

PLATE 239. *Painting by Franz Xavier Winterhalter.* 24 × 20 in. No. 2554.

EDWARD, DUKE OF KENT. 1767–1820.

Fourth son of George III: he served in the army and was appointed Commander-in-Chief in British North America in 1799 and Governor of Gilbraltar in 1802. The almost insane severity and finicky attention to minute details which prevented him from becoming a successful soldier, and his uncontrollable extravagance with money, were curiously at variance with his many admirable domestic virtues. He lived with Madame de St Laurent for nearly thirty years. Like two of his brothers, and for the same reason, he married after the death of Princess Charlotte, and he was the father of Queen Victoria. His humanity led him to undertake a vast deal of charitable work, and he gave support to Robert Owen's schemes for human betterment.

PLATE 240. *Painting by Sir William Beechey, 1818.* 29¼ × 24¼ in. No. 647.

QUEEN VICTORIA. 1819–1901.
She succeeded her uncle, William IV, to the throne in 1837. The strongest influences in her life were those of her mother, the Duchess of Kent, of her governess, the Baroness Lehzen, of her first Prime Minister, Lord Melbourne, and, above all, of her husband, Prince Albert. It was not until long after his death that her personal influence in politics was felt, but her devotion to duty, her strong Christian faith and her belief in the virtues of family life, set an example to the whole Empire.
PLATE 241. *Painting by Sir George Hayter.* 110½ × 68½ in. No. 1250.

PRINCE ALBERT FRANCIS CHARLES AUGUSTUS EMMANUEL OF SAXE-COBURG-GOTHA. 1819–1861.
Son of the Duke of Saxe-Coburg-Gotha, he married Queen Victoria in 1840. The distrust of his adopted countrymen for foreigners debarred him from an active part in politics. His influence on the Queen however was all-important, and lasted until her death. Considerably talented, he devoted himself largely to the patronage of science, the arts, building and social reform.
PLATE 242. *Painting by Franz Xavier Winterhalter.* 94 × 61 in. No. 237.

WILLIAM LAMB, 2ND VISCOUNT MELBOURNE. 1779–1848.
Though he was a great statesman, and Prime Minister from 1835 to 1841, showing himself liberal minded and well balanced during periods of seething unrest in the country, and though his fame was such that the great Australian city was named after him, it is as the devoted mentor of the young Queen Victoria that he is chiefly remembered. From the time of her accession to the throne at the age of eighteen until after her marriage he was always at her side, advising her with great wisdom and with paternal affection on the functions of a constitutional monarch, and guiding her through every difficulty.
PLATE 243. *Painting by John Partridge.* 49½ × 39½ in. No. 941.

CHARLES GREY, 2ND EARL GREY. 1764–1845.
In the 'Ministry of All the Talents' he was First Lord of the Admiralty and then Foreign Secretary, succeeding Fox as the leader of the Whigs. He remained out of office for twenty-four years until he became Prime Minister in 1831, when he introduced the Parliamentary Reform Bill: it was thrown out, but he carried the amended bill the following

year. His Cabinet split over the Irish question and in 1834 he resigned and retired from public life.

PLATE 244. *Painting after Lawrence.* $29\frac{1}{4} \times 24\frac{1}{2}$ in. No. 1190.

JOHN GEORGE LAMBTON, 1st EARL OF DURHAM. 1792–1840.

Statesman, and leader of an advanced section of the Whigs. He held ambassadorial posts in Russia and elsewhere, and during 1838 was High Commissioner for Canada. His imperious proceedings there were repudiated by the home government and he resigned, but the famous 'Durham Report' formed the basis of much future legislation. Undoubtedly he had great ability, but he was inordinately vain, turbulent and tactless, and as Lord Melbourne said, 'everybody must doubt whether there can be peace or harmony in a cabinet of which Lord Durham is a member'.

PLATE 245. *Painting by Thomas Phillips.* 36×28 in. No. 2547.

THOMAS ARNOLD. 1795–1842.

He was for fourteen years headmaster of Rugby and his reforms there not only changed the character of the school but made it the model on which the modern boarding school system is based. *Tom Brown's Schooldays*, by Thomas Hughes, gives a graphic, if slightly one-sided, picture of Rugby under his rule.

PLATE 246. *Painting by Thomas Phillips, 1839.* 48×39 in. No. 1998.

SIR ROBERT PEEL, BART. 1788–1850.

Chief Secretary for Ireland, 1812–18; Home Secretary under Liverpool and under Wellington; Prime Minister in 1834–5 and from 1841 to 1846. He was responsible for much important legislation such as the reform of the criminal laws, and for the formation of the Metropolitan Police Force, and the reorganisation of the banking system. Even in opposition, from 1835 till 1841, he was a formidable power, and he gathered round him a number of brilliant and progressive men, welding them into a 'Conservative' party. He had an inviolable sense of public duty and the courage to change his policy to meet changing conditions, as when he introduced the Catholic Emancipation Bill in 1829, accepted the Reform Act of 1832, and carried the repeal of the Corn Laws in 1846, although this inevitably led to a split in his party and his fall from office. He made a fine collection of paintings many of which are now in the National Gallery.

PLATE 247. *Painting by John Linnell, 1838.* $17\frac{3}{4} \times 14\frac{1}{2}$ in. No. 772.

HENRY JOHN TEMPLE, 3RD VISCOUNT PALMERSTON. 1784–1865.

From 1809, for nearly twenty years, he was Secretary of State for War: from 1830 to 1841 and from 1846 to 1851 he was Foreign Secretary. His belief that a determined threat, backed by a show of force, was almost invariably the surest way of maintaining peace was in a measure justified by his many brilliant successes, such as, among other things, the creation of Belgian independence, the breaking of absolutist power in Spain and Portugal, and the protection of Turkey from Russian aggression. Had he been more attended to during the negotiations leading to the Crimean War that too might perhaps have been avoided. For ten years, from 1855 till his death, he was Prime Minister. An indomitable nationalism was his ruling passion: he strove always to increase the power and prestige of Engand as 'the champion of justice and right', and in his remarkably high-handed, arrogant way he succeeded, winning at the same time great popularity at home.

PLATE 248. *Painting by John Partridge, 1846.* 36 × 28¾ in. No. 1025.

SYDNEY SMITH. 1771–1845.

Canon of St Paul's Cathedral and a member of the Whig circle at Holland House; his conversational powers and exuberant wit made him one of the most brilliant figures in London. His *Letters of Peter Plymley* are an energetic plea for Catholic emancipation in the name of common justice and common sense.

PLATE 249. *Painting by Henry Perronet Briggs.* 49½ × 39½ in. No. 1475.

ELIZABETH FRY (NÉE GURNEY). 1780–1845.

She came of a Norfolk Quaker family and, appalled by the conditions of women prisoners in Newgate, devoted her life to prison reform and to alleviating the hardships endured by convicts under sentence of transportation.

PLATE 250. *Painting after C. R. Leslie.* 8¼ × 6½ in. No. 898.

SIR JOHN FRANKLIN. 1786–1847.

He fought as a naval officer at Copenhagen (1801) and Trafalgar (1805), but is remembered for his heroic Arctic explorations. He and the crews of the *Erebus* and *Terror* perished on an expedition, which he commanded, to discover the North-West Passage round the north of Canada to the Pacific.

PLATE 251. *Painting by Thomas Phillips.* 29½ × 24¾ in. No. 903.

MICHAEL FARADAY. 1791–1867.
It is no exaggeration to say that his discoveries form the basis of modern physics. His series of *Experimental Researches on Electricity* made known new ideas in electro-magnetism. He made the first battery and the first dynamo. His gift for popular exposition drew large audiences to his lectures at the Royal Institution.
PLATE 252. *Painting by Thomas Phillips, 1842.* $35\frac{1}{2} \times 27\frac{1}{2}$ in. No. 269.

SIR HUMPHRY DAVY, BART. 1778–1829.
He made important experiments in galvanism, chemistry and electricity, but is remembered chiefly for his investigations into the cause of explosions in coal-mines and the invention of the 'safety-lamp'.
PLATE 253. *Painting by Thomas Phillips.* 36×28 in. No. 2546.

GEORGE STEPHENSON. 1781–1848.
He constructed his first steam locomotive, to transport coal from Killingworth colliery to the coast, in 1814. Passengers were first carried on his Stockton and Darlington mineral railway, 1825. His famous 'Rocket' steam engine which ran at 30 m.p.h. in 1829, and the Liverpool and Manchester railway, opened in 1830, led to the tremendous development and speculation in the national railway system. Like Davy, and at about the same time, he invented a safety lamp for miners.
PLATE 254. *Painting by Henry William Pickersgill.* $44 \times 34\frac{1}{4}$ in. No. 410.

JOHN KEBLE. 1792–1866.
His assize sermon on 'National Apostasy', preached at St Mary's, Oxford, in 1833, caused Newman to describe him as the 'true and primary author of the Oxford movement', but whereas Newman and later Manning led a current of the movement to Rome, Keble and Pusey stood for Anglo-Catholicism within the established Church. He was the author of *The Christian Year* (1827), a collection of sacred poems which attained great popularity, and in which are such familiar hymns as *Bless'd are the pure in Heart*.
PLATE 255. *Drawing by George Richmond, 1863.* 24×18 in. No. 1043.

EDWARD BOUVERIE PUSEY. 1800–1882.
With Newman and Keble, he was a leader of the tractarian movement, attempting to prevent the spread of rationalism by an appeal to fundamental Christian principles. Many of his colleagues seceded to Rome

but he remained within the Anglican church reassuring waverers and labouring towards a union between the Church of England and the Church of Rome.

PLATE 256. *Drawing by George Richmond.* 26 × 21 in. No. 1059.

ROBERT OWEN. 1771–1858.

His zeal for social reform was realised in the spinning mills at New Lanark where he introduced better labour conditions and an advanced system of education for the local children. During the slump after 1815, his 'villages of co-operation' brought a measure of relief, and though his attempt to develop them into a general project for a new social order was a failure, his vision led eventually to the great Co-operative movements of the nineteenth century.

PLATE 257. *Drawing by 'S.B.', 1851.* 14 × 10 in. No. 328.

JOHN RUSKIN. 1819–1900.

An only child, brought up at home and subjected to the rigid evangelical puritanism of a mother, and the romanticism of a father, who both encouraged his precocity. He wrote the first volume of *Modern Painters* while still at Oxford. In the subsequent volumes, in *The Seven Lamps of Architecture, The Stones of Venice* and in his lectures he proceeded to establish the fundamental canons of art, moral and aesthetic, and the world accepted his dictatorship in all questions of taste in painting and architecture. He championed particularly Turner and the Pre-Raphaelites, fostered the 'Gothic revival', and was himself an accomplished artist though his drawings lack the outstanding quality of his prose writing. In middle age he turned to economics and social reform, and much of the theory embodied in *Unto this Last* and *Time and Tide* was also accepted in time. He was a munificent and discreet philanthropist.

PLATE 258. *Drawing by George Richmond.* 17 × 14 in. No. 1058.

THOMAS CARLYLE. 1795–1881.

Strongly influenced by his early German studies, particularly by Goethe, his intemperate and aggressive philosophy found utterance in historical narratives such as *The French Revolution* (1837), *Cromwell's Letters and Speeches* (1845) and *Frederick II* (1858–65), all of which illustrate his belief that the history of the world may be found in the biographies of heroes, and all of which are written in magnificent rhythmic prose.

PLATE 259. *Painting by Sir John Everett Millais.* 45½ × 34½ in. No. 968.

JOHN STUART MILL. 1806–1873.

A philosopher and political economist who started in the Jeremy Bentham utilitarian school, but, in his *Principles of Political Economy* (1848), showed a trend towards liberal socialism. His essay *On Liberty* (1859) is his masterpiece.

PLATE 260. *Painting by George Frederic Watts, 1873.* 25½ × 20½ in. No. 1009.

THOMAS BABINGTON MACAULAY, 1ST BARON MACAULAY. 1800–1859.

Whig statesman and historian famous also for his verse, his essays and his formidable conversation. His great unfinished work, *The History of England from the Accession of James II* (1849–61), though biased and containing inaccuracies, must be reckoned as a literary masterpiece. Also very popular was his *Lays of Ancient Rome*, published in 1842.

PLATE 261. *Painting by Sir Francis Grant.* 11¼ × 9¼ in. No. 453.

MARY ANN CROSS (NÉE EVANS). 'GEORGE ELIOT'. 1819–1880.

She was one of the great Victorian novelists, her work including *Adam Bede* (1859), *The Mill on the Floss* (1860) and *Middlemarch* (1872), with characters drawn from the rural life of Warwickshire. Her emphasis was on moral issues and the power of intimate grief to purify the commonplace.

PLATE 262. *Drawing by Sir Frederick William Burton, 1865.* 20¼ × 15 in. No. 669.

MRS ELIZABETH CLEGHORN GASKELL (NÉE STEVENSON). 1810–1865.

The wife of a Manchester clergyman, she made the social evils of the industrial districts the main theme of her novels, of which the best known is *Mary Barton* (1848). *Cranford* (1853) is an idyllic account of life in an English village and her *Life of Charlotte Brontë* (1857) is among the masterpieces of English biography.

PLATE 263. *Drawing by George Richmond, 1851.* 24½ × 18¾ in. No. 1720.

CHARLOTTE MARY YONGE. 1823–1901.

Her novels and historical romances are permeated by the High Church influence of the tractarians and especially Keble who was vicar of Hursley, the neighbouring parish to hers in Hampshire. The *Heir of Redclyffe* (1853) and *The Daisy Chain* (1856) were her most successful books; the financial profits from them were mostly devoted to missionary work.

PLATE 264. *Water-colour by George Richmond, 1844.* 21½ × 14¼ in. No. 2193.

EDWARD GEORGE EARLE LYTTON BULWER-LYTTON, 1ST BARON LYTTON. 1803–1873.

In spite of a crowded public life and a desperately unhappy home, he was able to produce a flow of essays, plays, poems, political treatises and a series of artificial but extremely popular romantic novels. Among these are *Eugene Aram* (1832), *The Last Days of Pompeii* (1832) and *Rienzi* (1835).

PLATE 265. *Water-colour by Alfred Edward Chalon.* 17½ × 13 in. No. 1099.

DANTE GABRIEL ROSSETTI. 1828–1882.

As a painter, as a poet, and as one of the Pre-Raphaelite Brotherhood his influence was decisive at a time when accepted idioms were becoming outworn and sterile. Some of his best-known poetry, including *The Blessed Damozel*, was written before he was twenty years old. One of his earliest paintings was the 'Ecce Ancilla Domini' which has a sentimental simplicity and is restrained in colour; in most of his pictures, and especially such as 'Monna Vanna' or 'The Beloved' there is, together with some exaggerated mannerisms, a sensuous magnificence of colour and design which finds an echo in his verse.

PLATE 266. *Drawing by himself, 1847.* 7¾ × 7 in. No. 857.

CHRISTINA GEORGINA ROSSETTI. 1830–1894.

A sister of Dante Gabriel and, like him, a highly gifted and precocious writer. Her poetry shows a strong sense of melody and is imbued with a spiritual and melancholy longing. Her finest poems are included in the volume first published, *Goblin Market and Other Poems* (1862). Later works include the series of sonnets of unhappy love, *Monna Innominata*, and a great number of devotional poems.

PLATE 267. *Drawing by Dante Gabriel Rossetti, 1877.* 16¾ × 19 in. No. 990.

ROBERT BROWNING. 1812–1889.

He was a poet whose absorbing interest lay in psychological analysis. His lyrical optimism, invigorated by the romance with Elizabeth

Barrett, was expressed in such outbursts as *Pippa Passes* and *Home Thoughts from Abroad*. His masterpiece, *The Ring and the Book* (1868–9) has for its subject an Italian murder story and is an extraordinary mixture of prolixity, technical virtuosity and dramatic effect.

PLATE 268. *Drawing by Field Talfourd, 1859.* 25¼ × 17½ in. No. 1269.

ELIZABETH BARRETT BROWNING. 1806–1861.

She was reading Greek and writing poetry at eight years old; at fifteen she suffered an accident which left her an invalid for the greater part of her life; at twenty she published the *Essay on Mind*. She was forty when she met Browning and wrote *Sonnets from the Portuguese*, the finest of all her verses, telling of her love and of her release from the thralldom of her father. After her marriage she lived mostly in Italy, and her best-known works from this period are *Casa Guidi Windows* and *Aurora Leigh*. Hawthorne described her as 'a pale small person, scarcely embodied at all'.

PLATE 269. *Drawing by Field Talfourd, 1859.* 24 × 17½ in. No. 322.

THE BRONTË SISTERS. ANNE. 1820–1849. EMILY JANE. 1818–1848. CHARLOTTE (MRS A. B. NICHOLLS). 1816–1855.

Brought up, without a mother, in the solitude and wildness of the Yorkshire moors, they discovered that each was secretly engaged in literary activity, and in 1846, under the pseudonyms of Currer, Ellis and Acton Bell they published a volume of their combined poems. There followed during the next two years a novel by each of them. Anne's *Agnes Grey* made little impression; Emily's *Wuthering Heights* achieved a bewildered notoriety; Charlotte's first novel had been refused, but *Jane Eyre* gained immediate success, though her joy at this was shattered by the death soon after of both her sisters and her brother Patrick Branwell. The work of all three sisters shows unusually vivid power of imagination and is typical of the heightened romanticism guyed by Thackeray and others.

PLATE 270. *Painting by Patrick Branwell Brontë.* 35 × 29½ in. No. 1725.

WILLIAM MAKEPEACE THACKERAY. 1811–1863.

Having as a young man disposed of a comfortable inheritance from his father he first thought to earn his living by drawing. Turning gradually to writing and starting with miscellaneous hack work he steadily progressed until he rivalled even Dickens in popularity. His first decided success was with the 'Snob Papers' contributed to the newly founded *Punch*; with the serial publication of *Vanity Fair* during 1847/8 he began to be recognised as one of the foremost novelists, and the later novels, such as *The History of Pendennis*, *The History of Henry Esmond*, *The Newcomes* and *The Virginians* secured his lasting fame.

PLATE 271. *Painting by Samuel Laurence.* $29\frac{1}{4} \times 24\frac{3}{4}$ in. No. 725.

ANTHONY TROLLOPE. 1815–1882.

He created the county of Barsetshire, its cathedral town of Barchester, its small towns and villages, its churches, castles and cottages, and he peopled it with characters so various and so convincing as once met can never be forgotten. The unworldly Mr Harding, for example, or the redoubtable Mrs Proudie, or Archdeacon Grantly, show that, like Jane Austen, he had the humorous intuition and the swift, sure touch that can bring people vividly to life without seeming to go below the surface. He began life as a Post Office official: once started on a career of writing he disciplined himself to produce novels with ease and regularity. In his autobiography he maintained that the Palliser series of parliamentary novels, rather than those of Barsetshire, was his best work, but later generations of readers have thought otherwise.

PLATE 272. *Painting by Samuel Laurence, 1865.* $23\frac{1}{2} \times 19\frac{3}{4}$ in. No. 1680.

CHARLES DICKENS. 1812–1870.

His position among the great novelists of the world is assured by such books as *The Pickwick Papers*, *Oliver Twist*, *Nicholas Nickleby* and *David Copperfield*. Most of his work appeared in serial form and was eagerly awaited, month by month, by multitudes of readers. The perennial popularity of his writing is largely due to his skill in combining humour with tenderness and in bringing his characters vividly to life by the emphasis of idiosyncracies; but his historical significance lies rather in the power he had of awakening the public conscience to a sense of social evils and abuses.

PLATE 273. *Painting by Daniel Maclise, 1839.* $35\frac{1}{4} \times 27$ in. No. 1172.

ALFRED TENNYSON, 1ST BARON TENNYSON. 1809–1892.

His poetry, with Browning's, may be said to have dominated the mid-Victorian era. It shows a return to the classical perfection of the eighteenth century allied to the romanticism of the early nineteenth, and his appointment as poet laureate, in succession to Wordsworth, in 1850, was one of the more discerning acts of Queen Victoria's reign. *Maud, In Memoriam* and *Idylls of the King* are outstanding in an immense body of work.

PLATE 274. *Painting by Samuel Laurence.* 26¾ × 22¾ in. No. 2460.

ALGERNON CHARLES SWINBURNE. 1837–1909.

With *Atalanta in Calydon*, published in 1865, he won a success which developed into noisy notoriety with the publication of *Poems and Ballads* the following year. It is said that Mazzini admonished him to abjure this 'love frenzy' and devote his powers to the glorification of Republican ideals: hence, among other things, *Songs before Sunrise*, published in 1871. His poetry, strongly influenced by the French, especially Baudelaire and Victor Hugo, shows astonishing virtuosity in its melody and rhythm and in its curious patterning of repetition and alliteration. *A Century of Roundels*, published in 1883, led Tennyson to call him 'a reed through which all things blow into music'.

PLATE 275. *Painting by George Frederic Watts, 1865.* 25½ × 20½ in. No. 1542.

WILLIAM EWART GLADSTONE. 1809–1898.

Four times Liberal Prime Minister between 1868 and 1894. He was also a classical scholar and mathematician, outstanding as a financier, a brilliant Chancellor of the Exchequer and a very great orator with power to hold the mob in thrall. Although his staunchest supporters came from the aggressive non-conformity of the North, his own life was stabilised by a devout Anglicanism which served him as a guide in every political and moral judgment. During his administration acts tending to free trade and to extend the franchise were passed, also important measures of reform in England and Ireland, but he was repeatedly defeated over home rule for Ireland for which he laboured ardently during the last ten years of his working life.

PLATE 276. *Painting by Sir John Everett Millais, 1879.* 50 × 36½ in. No. 3637.

BENJAMIN DISRAELI, 1st EARL OF BEACONSFIELD. 1804–1881.

In an era and a country hostile to his oriental flamboyance of speech and dress and distrustful of his wit, he succeeded in becoming one of the greatest Tory parliamentary leaders. He was twice Prime Minister, and his public career can be seen as a long duel with Gladstone in which the antagonists were not ill matched. The outstanding feature of his government was its imperialism—the Queen's acceptance of the title of 'Empress of India', the purchase of the Suez Canal shares, and the diplomatic triumph of the Congress of Berlin. He was also a writer of considerable power and much light is thrown on English politics by his many novels, which include *Coningsby, Tancred* and *Lothair*.

PLATE 277. *Painting by Sir John Everett Millais, 1881.* 50 × 36 in. No. 3241.

RICHARD COBDEN. 1804–1865.
The leader, with John Bright, of the Free Trade movement. For eight years indefatigable at the head of the Anti-Corn Law League, slowly but surely he won ground, broke up a strong administration under Peel, who was converted, and finally secured the repeal of the corn laws in 1846. With the same determination he performed the immense labour of negotiating the commercial treaty with France which led to vastly improved relations. Always strongly against armed intervention abroad, he ran counter to popular feeling by opposing the policy of the Crimean War.

PLATE 278. *Painting by Lowes Cato Dickinson, 1869.* 71½ × 47½ in. No. 316.

JOHN BRIGHT. 1811–1889.
Champion of Free Trade. He worked with Richard Cobden for the repeal of the corn laws, and in support of a non-intervention policy. Together they represent the emergence of the manufacturing class as a political power. His ultimate goal was always the improvement of conditions for the masses and he approved the extension of the franchise, but he opposed factory reform and education bills, not deeming parental legislation the most proper way of dealing with such things. He was an eloquent speaker and coined memorable phrases; even when well past his prime his hostility to Irish home rule seriously damaged Gladstone's cause.

PLATE 279. *Painting by Walter William Ouless, 1879.* 48½ × 38¾ in. No. 817.

ROBERT ARTHUR TALBOT GASCOYNE-CECIL, 3RD MARQUESS OF SALISBURY. 1830–1903.
Three times Prime Minister, he directed foreign policy for most of the period 1878–1902. His monumental wisdom and skill in diplomacy

repeatedly steered the country away from imminent danger of war, but the Jameson raid of 1896 led to a situation beyond his control, and finally to the Boer War. In home affairs his conservatism was tempered by his readiness to respect the force of changing conditions and modes of thought; in private life he was a student of science and theology, and religiously devout. His fundamental simplicity and integrity inspired a trust in his patriotism which transcended party politics.

PLATE 280. *Painting by George Frederic Watts, 1884.* 25½ × 20½ in. No. 1349.

JOHN LAIRD MAIR LAWRENCE, 1st BARON LAWRENCE. 1811–1879.

His energy and determination, grasp of detail and understanding of native affairs made him one of our finest administrators, and under him the Punjab was so well controlled that he was able to send large forces, transports and stores to the help of the army at Delhi; according to Canning it was mainly thanks to him that England kept her hold over Upper India. He was Viceroy from 1863 to 1869, a period for the most part of peace and recuperation after the ravages of the Mutiny.

PLATE 281. *Painting by George Frederic Watts, 1862.* 23½ × 19½ in. No. 1005.

CHARLES GEORGE GORDON. 1833–1885.

He fought with distinction in the Crimean and Chinese wars, and in command of a heterogeneous little army did brilliant work in suppressing the Taipon rebellion, earning the name of 'Chinese Gordon'. As Governor of the Egyptian Equatorial Provinces and of the Soudan he combated disease, corruption and the slave trade and established an amazing personal ascendancy. He resigned in 1880. In 1884 the British Government decided to abandon the Soudan and sent him out again to bring away the garrisons. But it neglected to take any of the steps he declared necessary and in consequence he was cut off and besieged in Khartoum, and the expedition which was sent to his relief, only after months of procrastination and as a result of popular clamour, arrived too late to save his life.

PLATE 282. *Water-colour by Lady Abercromby.* 23½ × 19½ in. No. 1772.

SIR RICHARD FRANCIS BURTON. 1821–1890.

During a lifetime of exploration, mainly in Africa and America, he made his celebrated journey to Mecca, disguised as an Afghan. Like

Livingstone later, he set out to explore the sources of the Nile, and travelling with J. H. Speke discovered Lake Tanganyika. He learnt thirty-five oriental languages and dialects, translated *The Arabian Nights*, and wrote a large number of books about his travels.

PLATE 283. *Painting by Frederic, Lord Leighton, 1876.* 23½ × 19½ in. No. 1070.

DAVID LIVINGSTONE. 1813–1873.

He first went to Africa as a missionary in 1840 and thereafter most of his life was spent in hazardous and unhealthy exploration. He contrived somehow to survive the menace of hostile Boers, Portuguese and Arab slave-raiders, of cannibals, fever and tsetse fly, and he won the confidence and affection of many native tribes. His journeys took him to the Zambesi and the Victoria Falls, to Lake Ngami, Lake Nyasa and Lake Tanganyika. Pursuing his great wish to discover the sources of the Nile when he was unfit for further travel he perished in the Ilala country.

PLATE 284. *Painting by Frederick Havill.* 41½ × 32¾ in. No. 1040.

CECIL JOHN RHODES. 1853–1902.

As a youth he went to South Africa and he joined the rush to the diamond fields: he prospered exceedingly until, as head of De Beers Mines, he virtually controlled the industry. But his ideals were imperial rather than commercial and he dreamed of all Africa, from Cairo to the Cape, united under the British flag. In 1889 he conceived and organised the British South Africa Company to develop, in the first place, the territory named after him. He was Prime Minister of the Cape from 1890 to 1896. On his death before the age of fifty his fortune of some six million pounds was bequeathed to the public service, notably the foundation of the Rhodes scholarships at Oxford.

PLATE 285. *Painting by George Frederic Watts.* 33¾ × 26¾ in. No. 1407.

CHARLES ROBERT DARWIN. 1809–1882.

The great naturalist whose name will be forever linked with his theory of evolution. His post as naturalist in the five-year voyage of the survey ship, H.M.S. *Beagle* (1831–6) led him to the revolutionary conclusions which found shape in his *Origin of Species by Means of Natural Selection* (1859), a book which aroused immense controversy, mainly because it conflicted with the Book of Genesis.

PLATE 286. *Painting by the Hon. John Collier.* 49½ × 38 in. No. 1024.

THOMAS HENRY HUXLEY. 1825–1895.

His marine research work as assistant-surgeon in H.M.S. *Rattlesnake* (1846–50) began a career which ended in his becoming one of the outstanding scientific figures of the century, ensuring the recognition of Darwin's discoveries, and contributing much original biological research in the field of anthropology and organic evolution. He coined the word 'agnostic' to express his religious views.

PLATE 287. *Painting by The Hon. John Collier, 1883.* 50 × 40 in. No. 3168.

JOSEPH LISTER, 1st BARON LISTER. 1827–1912.

While practising as a surgeon he continued with inspired research work and discovered the principle of sterilisation. He introduced antiseptic treatment for wounds and in the operating theatre, thereby immensely reducing suffering and fatalities and increasing the potentialities of surgery. This one discovery marks such a great advance in medical science that it has overshadowed other original and important work done by him.

PLATE 288. *Plaster bust by Sir Thomas Brock.* 29½ in. high. No. 1958.

FLORENCE NIGHTINGALE. 1820–1910.

In the Crimean War, with a small party of nurses and working against tremendous opposition, she reduced the high mortality rate due to insanitary hospital conditions at Scutari where her visits to the wards earned her the title of 'the lady of the lamp'. With weakened health but unimpaired energy she devoted the rest of her long life chiefly to the reform of nursing and of sanitation.

PLATE 289. *Bronze bust by Sir John Robert Steel, 1862.* 28 in. high. No. 1748.

WILLIAM THOMSON, 1st BARON KELVIN. 1824–1907.

At the age of twenty-two he was appointed Professor of Natural Philosophy at Glasgow university where he was a dominating figure for fifty-three years. His especial fields were in thermo-electricity, the design of marine instruments and the Atlantic submarine cable. His physical laboratory was the first to be established in Great Britain.

PLATE 290. *Painting by Elizabeth Thomson King, 1887.* 20½ × 15¾ in. No. 1708.

JOHN FREDERICK DENISON MAURICE. 1805–1872.
An Anglican theologian and Christian socialist who, reacting to
sectarian discord in his youth at home, tried to show that the only hope
for the Protestant, and ultimately the Christian faith, lay in complete
unity. A strong believer in practical Christianity, he founded the
Working Men's College now at Camden Town.
PLATE 291. *Painting by Samuel Laurence.* 36¾ × 32¾ in. No. 1042.

ANTHONY ASHLEY-COOPER, 7TH EARL OF
SHAFTESBURY. 1801–1885.
The leader of many social reform movements, such as the reform of
the lunacy acts, the care of destitute children, the protection of chimney-
climbing boys, the improvement of housing, the regulation of working
hours in factories and mines and the exclusion of women and children
from work underground, all of which at first aroused fierce hostility
from his own wealthy aristocratic class and from *laissez-faire* politicians.
He was moved by a strong Evangelical fervour, was the champion of
the 'ragged schools', and supported Biblical societies and missionary
work among the poor.
PLATE 292. *Painting by George Frederic Watts.* 23½ × 19½ in. No. 1012.

WILLIAM BOOTH. 1829–1912.
Beginning with mission work in the East End of London, he later
founded the Salvation Army which owes its impetus to the enthusiasm
and organising skill of 'General' Booth, his wife Catherine, and their
son and daughter.
PLATE 293. *Painting by David N. Ingles.* 35¼ × 27¼ in. No. 2042.

JOHN HENRY NEWMAN. 1801–1890.
Vicar of St Mary's, Oxford, 1828–43, and a leader of the Oxford
tractarian movement, he joined the Church of Rome in 1845. During
the following years he established the Oratories at Birmingham and
London. He became a cardinal in 1879. His best-remembered literary
works are the *Apologia pro Vita sua*, his defence against Kingsley's attack
on Roman Catholicism (1864), the hymn *Lead Kindly Light* (1833),
and *The Dream of Gerontius* (1865), which was set to music by Elgar.
PLATE 294. *Painting by Emmeline Deane, 1889.* 43¾ × 34¾. No. 1022.

EDWARD HENRY MANNING. 1808–1892.
A clergyman of the Church of England for twenty years, he became
a Roman Catholic in 1851, and later succeeded Cardinal Wiseman as

Archbishop of Westminster, becoming a cardinal himself in 1875. He ardently defended the doctrine of papal infallibility in his *True Story of the Vatican Council*. Despite accusations of ambition, he was a champion of the poor and was tireless in exposing social evils.

PLATE 295. *Painting by George Frederic Watts, 1882.* 35½ × 27½ in. No. 1008.

CHARLES KINGSLEY. 1819–1875.

An Anglican clergyman, he championed Christian socialism in his sermons and writings, notably *Alton Locke* (1850) and *Yeast* (1851). His very successful stories for children include *Westward Ho!* (1855), *The Water Babies* (1863) and *Hereward the Wake* (1866).

PLATE 296. *Painting by Lowes Cato Dickinson, 1862.* 35½ in. diameter. No. 2525.

CHARLES READE. 1814–1884.

A novelist and playwright, he was profoundly stirred by contemporary humanitarian movements, especially on behalf of criminals and lunatics. However, his masterpiece *The Cloister and the Hearth* (1861) is set in fifteenth-century Europe and is among the finest of English historical novels.

PLATE 297. *Painting attributed to C. Mercier.* 43¼ × 55¼ in. No. 2281.

WILLIAM HOLMAN-HUNT. 1827–1910.

The leading spirit of the 'Pre-Raphaelite Brotherhood', he remained true to its principles throughout his long life. In pursuit of verisimilitude for his paintings of Biblical subjects he made journeys to the Holy Land. His painting 'The Light of the World', finished in 1854, is now at Keble College, Oxford: fifty years later he painted a larger version of it which is in St Paul's Cathedral.

PLATE 298. *Painting by John Ballantyne.* 28 × 24 in. No. 2555.

SIR EDWIN HENRY LANDSEER. 1802–1873.

An infant prodigy who by the age of ten years showed skill in drawing, etching and painting, and first exhibited at the Royal Academy at thirteen. He was a successful portrait painter, particularly good with children, but he is best known as a painter of animals; his works enjoyed an immense popularity due, perhaps, to their anthropomorphic sentimentality. 'Dignity and Impudence' (1839) and 'The Monarch of the Glen' (1851) were among his most popular paintings, and the bronze lions in Trafalgar Square are his best-known works in sculpture. PLATE 299. *Painting by John Ballantyne.* 30½ × 43½ in. No. 835.

SIR EDWARD COLEY BURNE-JONES, BART. 1833–1898.

His lifelong friendship with William Morris began at Oxford; he soon came under the influence of Ruskin and Rossetti who encouraged him to turn artist. His early water-colours are perhaps his best memorial, but the bulk of his work was in oil, the subjects drawn mainly from Arthurian romance, medieval ballads and classical mythology. He made a great many designs for stained glass windows, some of which were executed by William Morris, and for tapestry and needlework, and he illustrated the Chaucer printed at Morris's Kelmscott Press. PLATE 300. *Painting by Sir Philip Burne-Jones, 1898.* 29½ × 21 in. No. 1864.

SIR JOHN EVERETT MILLAIS, BART. 1829–1896.

He showed a precocious skill in drawing and painting, and as a boy carried off all the prizes from the Academy schools. About 1848 he met Holman-Hunt and together they started the Pre-Raphaelite movement: they were very soon joined by Rossetti and the other four members of the Brotherhood. In 1850 his painting 'Christ in the House of His Parents' was condemned by Dickens in *Household Words* as 'mean, odious, revolting and repulsive', but was warmly championed by Ruskin. His painting ranges from the rich, imaginative, early works, such as 'Ophelia', to fashionable portraits and to popular story pictures such as 'The Boyhood of Raleigh'. He became President of the Royal Academy in 1896. PLATE 301. *Painting by George Frederic Watts, 1871.* 25½ × 20½ in. No. 3552.

SIR CHARLES HALLÉ. 1819–1895.

Pianist and conductor. Born in Westphalia, he spent much of his early working life in Paris, where his friends included Chopin, Liszt, Berlioz and Wagner. The Revolution of 1848 drove him to England where he settled for the rest of his life, choosing Manchester as his home and founding there the celebrated Hallé orchestra. PLATE 302. *Painting by George Frederic Watts.* 29¼ × 19¼ in. No. 1004.

ISABELLA MARY BEETON (NÉE MAYSON). 1836–1865.
She studied the piano in Heidelberg before her marriage in 1856 to Samuel Beeton, a publisher. Though she lived only another nine years, she had four children, wrote articles for the *Englishwoman's Domestic Magazine* and published that indispensable monument of domestic erudition, her *Book of Household Management*.
PLATE 303. *A photograph.* 7¼ × 5½ in. No. 2539.

JOHANNA MARIA (JENNY) LIND (MRS LIND-GOLDSCHMIDT). 1820–1887.
A soprano of a brilliant and thrilling quality, especially in the upper register. She left the operatic stage in 1849, after attaining a popularity unrivalled since the days of Mrs Siddons, and confined her singing to concerts and oratorio. She endowed a number of charities and scholarships. Known, from the country of her birth, as 'The Swedish Nightingale', she became a naturalised British subject.
PLATE 304. *Painting by Eduard Magnus.* 46½ × 37¼ in. No. 3801.

SIR WILLIAM SCHWENK GILBERT. 1836–1911.
Author of a vast number of plays, librettos, stories and verses, often illustrated by himself. In peculiarly felicitous combination with the music of Sullivan his inimitable accomplishment as a versifier, his deft precision of aim as a satirist and the humour 'based on a grave and quasi-respectful treatment of the ludicrous' which we call 'Gilbertian', ensured the undying popularity of the Savoy operas: their initial success also owed much to his originality and skill as a theatrical producer.
PLATE 305. *Painting by Frank Holl, 1886.* 39½ × 49½ in. No. 2911.

SIR ARTHUR SEYMOUR SULLIVAN. 1842–1900.
Composer whose collaboration with W. S. Gilbert as librettist is immortalised in the triumphant series of comic operas produced in partnership with R. d'Oyly Carte, first at the Opera Comique, then at the Savoy theatre specially built for the purpose. He also composed much 'serious' music, but his constant longing to devote more time to it was largely frustrated by the importunities of Gilbert and d'Oyly Carte, by the overwhelming success of the Savoy operas and by his own irrepressible natural genius in that *genre*: time and continuous repetition have not lessened the popularity of these operas, but his grand opera

233

Ivanhoe and his oratorios, though successful at the time, are now seldom heard.

PLATE 306. *Painting by Sir John Everett Millais, 1888.* 45½ × 34¼ in. No. 1325.

FREDERICK GUSTAVUS BURNABY. 1842–1885.

Traveller, soldier and balloonist of great linguistic abilities and immense physique. *The Ride to Khiva*, his account of his famous winter ride across Russia to investigate the Russian government's refusal to admit Europeans into Central Asia, was published in 1877 and became highly popular. He joined the expedition intended for the relief of General Gordon and was killed on the way to Khartoum.

PLATE 307. *Painting by James Tissot, 1870.* 19½ × 23½ in. No. 2642.

WILLIAM GILBERT GRACE. 1848–1915.

A medical practitioner by profession, he was the most famous of all cricketers. He twice captained the English team and he made one hundred and twenty-six centuries.

PLATE 308. *Painting by an unknown artist.* 35½ × 27½ in. No. 2112.

FREDERIC LEIGHTON, 1ST BARON LEIGHTON. 1830–1896.

He was President of the Royal Academy from 1878 till his death, and the personification of the 'Victorian Olympus'. His painting 'Cimabue's Madonna Carried in Procession through the Streets of Florence' (1855) was an immediate success and was bought by Queen Victoria. His sculpture 'An Athlete Struggling with a Python' (1877) and his painting 'The Bath of Psyche' (1890), both in the Tate Gallery, are typical of his work and reflect his cosmopolitan upbringing and art training.

PLATE 309. *Painting by George Frederic Watts, 1881.* 38½ × 29½ in. No. 1049.

GEORGE FREDERIC WATTS. 1817–1904.

A painter and sculptor whose fine gifts and tremendous industry were dedicated to an ideal of artistic achievement irrespective of worldly success. As a painter of allegorical pictures conceived on a heroic scale his declared aim was to elevate the mind by nobility of line and colour. As a portrait painter he showed a reticent distinction in keeping with the high moral earnestness of so many of the notable contemporaries whose portraits he intended as a gift to the nation. Some fifty of them are in the National Portrait Gallery.

PLATE 310. *Painting by himself.* 25 × 20 in. No. 1406.

WILLIAM MORRIS. 1834–1896.

His imperative creative urge was never canalised, and a perpetual search for new mediums of artistic expression led him to turn from architecture to painting; to writing—prose, verse and translations from Greek, Latin, French and Icelandic; to ecclesiastical and domestic interior decorating; to designing and manufacturing—furniture, textiles, wall-papers and the like; to manuscript illuminating; to printing and book design. He also took a part in public affairs as a socialist leader, and much of his political theory is contained in *News from Nowhere* which depicts a romantic communist Utopia. But behind his diversity was the constant conviction that the principles of art must be governed by moral, social and political doctrines. He was constant also in turning to medieval life, art and literature for his inspiration.

PLATE 311. *Painting by George Frederic Watts, 1880.* 25½ × 20½ in. No. 1078.

MATTHEW ARNOLD. 1822–1888.

Son of the famous headmaster of Rugby; an Inspector of Schools and Professor of Poetry at Oxford. As a poet he occasionally reached the level of the great Victorians, and as a literary critic he vigorously attacked the Philistine and was consistently original and inspiring.

PLATE 312. *Painting by George Frederic Watts.* 26 × 20½ in. No. 1000.

SAMUEL BUTLER. 1835–1902.

After sheep farming in New Zealand he came home, and with brief spells of painting and composing, devoted the rest of his life to satirical writing. Victorian 'morality'—he would have called it cant—the authorship of the *Odyssey*, and the family were among the many targets of his wit. His *Erewhon* was published in 1872, *The Way of all Flesh* in 1903.

PLATE 313. *Painting by Charles Gogin, 1896.* 27 × 20½in. No. 1599.

WILLIAM HENRY HUDSON. 1841–1922.

When as a boy he 'ran wild in a wild land', the South American pampas, he began a life-long study of nature—bird life particularly. In 1869 he came to England where poverty kept him caged up in London boarding houses till he was befriended by Grey, and in 1901 a civil list pension brought relief. To the sensitive observation of his naturalist works is added, in the autobiographical *Far Away and Long Ago*, a protest against the crimes of 'civilisation'. The best known of his romantic stories is *Green Mansions*. The bird sanctuary in Hyde Park was opened in 1925 as a memorial to him.

PLATE 314. *Painting by Sir William Rothenstein.* 20¼ × 16¼ in. No. 1965.

SIR HENRY RIDER HAGGARD. 1856–1925.

Although he served under Bulwer and Shepstone in South Africa, was a practical agriculturist and the author of *The Farmer's Year Book* and *Rural England*, and a member of Commissions and Committees concerned with Dominion affairs, he is remembered chiefly for his novels. These were of many kinds, from the fantastic to the historical, but most enduringly popular are the vivid and exciting romances such as *King Solomon's Mines* and *She*.

PLATE 315. *Painting by John Pettie, 1889.* 30 × 25 in. No. 2801.

ROBERT LOUIS BALFOUR STEVENSON. 1850–1894.

Ill health prevented him from following the family profession of engineering, or from practising as a lawyer though he was called to the bar in Edinburgh; he was therefore able to devote himself to his true *métier* of writing, and with indomitable persistence laboured to perfect the meticulously polished literary style of his essays. He travelled constantly in search of health and finally settled in Samoa where he became known to the natives as Tusitala—teller of tales. They are many and include *Treasure Island*, *Kidnapped* and *The Strange Case of Dr Jekyll and Mr Hyde*, and despite his pitiful physical condition they are told with triumphant zest.

PLATE 316. *Painting by Sir William Blake Richmond, 1887.* 28 × 21 in. No. 1028.

GEORGE MEREDITH. 1828–1909.

One of his early novels, *Evan Harrington*, was inspired by the history of his remarkable grandfather, 'The Great Mel', tailor of Portsmouth, around whom he spun a tale of purest comedy. The 'Comic Spirit' was ever at his elbow, and as his powers of insight and analysis developed and his range and complexity increased, was constantly invoked to keep the balance true and to deal summarily with the least threat of sentimentality, as, for example, in *The Egoist*. Until the publication of *Diana of the Crossways* in 1885 his importance as a novelist and as a poet was recognised only by writers and critics. Much of his verse—*Love in the Valley* or *The Woods of Westermain* may be cited—has great beauty, and his prose, rich and individual, has a fine balance and rhythm, but he makes considerable demands on the reader and he never appealed to a wide public. Eventually he came to be looked upon with reverence as the greatest literary figure of the time.

PLATE 317. *Painting by George Frederic Watts, 1893.* $28\frac{1}{4} \times 20\frac{1}{4}$ in. No. 1543.

THOMAS HARDY. 1840–1928.

Trained, and for a time practising, as an architect, by 1870 he had settled to writing as a career, and although his strongest urge was to write poetry and he regarded prose fiction merely as a means of earning a living, the many novels he produced during the next twenty years, particularly those dealing with the rural society of his Wessex, place him with the greatest English authors. They include *Under the Greenwood Tree, Tess of the D'Urbervilles* and *Jude the Obscure.* Early in the 1890's he was able to give up other work and concentrate on poetry, and his major work, the epic drama *The Dynasts*, was published in three parts from 1903 to 1908, to be followed by several volumes of lyrics.

PLATE 318. *Painting by William Strang, 1893.* 17×15 in. No. 2929.

MARY AUGUSTA WARD (MRS HUMPHREY WARD, NÉE ARNOLD). 1851–1920.

'The most impressive woman writer of her time', she wrote a steady run of solid novels. One of them, *Robert Elsmere*, in which she expressed doubts on miracles, attained undeserved notoriety and drew a reply from Gladstone. A pioneer social worker, she succeeded in wakening public conscience to the need for special schools for crippled children.

PLATE 319. *Painting by Julian Russell Story, 1889.* $17\frac{1}{2} \times 14$ in. No. 2650.

JOSEPH RUDYARD KIPLING. 1865–1936.

Others have written of India with greater depth, but none have matched the brilliance of his Indian tales. Though he spoke nobly in verse, he was at his best in short story form. The range of his genius is vastly greater than the mood of imperialism with which it has been identified, and though he was sometimes caustic, works like *Puck of Pook's Hill*, the *Jungle Books* or the *Just So Stories* were written from love and have become beloved.

PLATE 320. *Painting by Sir Philip Burne-Jones, 1899.* $29\frac{1}{2} \times 24\frac{1}{2}$ in. No. 1863.

OSCAR FINGAL O'FLAHERTIE WILLS WILDE.
1854–1900.
As an undergraduate at Magdalen College, Oxford, he founded the
aesthetic cult which was pilloried by Gilbert in *Patience*. He was a
scintillating wit and conversationalist, and his comedies, such as *Lady
Windermere's Fan* (1892), *A Woman of No Importance* (1893) and *The
Importance of Being Ernest* (1895) brought back to the English stage
some of the sparkle of Sheridan and the Restoration dramatists. His
trial and imprisonment provoked the anguished *Ballad of Reading Gaol*
(1898) and *De Profundis* (1905)
PLATE 321. *Caricature by 'Ape', 1884.* 12¼ × 7¼ in. No. 3653.

CHARLES LUTWIDGE DODGSON. 'LEWIS
CARROLL'. 1832–1898.
A mathematics don at Oxford, hampered by excessive shyness and
a stammer, but also the author of *Alice's Adventures in Wonderland* and
Alice Through the Looking-Glass. Various explanations of his complex
personality have been suggested, but the question seems irrelevant in
relation to these stories which when all is said, remain, with their simple
and benign absurdity, the most delightful and lastingly popular of all
books for children.
PLATE 322. *Caricature by Harry Furniss.* 8¼ × 5¼ in. No. 2609.

SIR JOHN TENNIEL. 1820–1914.
He is chiefly memorable for the illustrations, known to generations
of children, to *Alice's Adventures in Wonderland*, *Alice Through the
Looking-Glass* and *The Ingoldsby Legends*. After Leech's death in 1864,
he joined the staff of *Punch* and, for fifty years, produced their weekly
political cartoon.
PLATE 323. *Drawing by himself, 1889.* 8 × 6 in. No. 2818.

JAMES ABBOTT McNEILL WHISTLER. 1834–1903.
American by birth, he settled in Paris in 1855, and later in London
where many famous pictures such as the 'Nocturnes', 'Battersea
Bridge', 'The Artist's Mother' and the 'Portrait of Carlyle' were
painted. He was a great master of etching and in his plates, as in his
canvases, a Japanese influence can be felt. Thanks largely to his exhibitionism, mordant wit and gift for repartee, his libel action against Ruskin
in 1878 was the *cause celèbre* of the period.
PLATE 324. *Water-colour by Sir Leslie Ward.* 13¾ × 8½ in. No. 1700.

EDWARD LEAR. 1812–1888.

He began work as an ornithological draughtsman, producing the plates to *The Knowsley Menagerie* (1832–6) for the Earl of Derby, for whose grandchildren he wrote and illustrated the limericks published as *The Book of Nonsense* in 1846. He then devoted himself to travel and to painting water-colour landscapes of much decorative and topographic interest, mainly on the Mediterranean shores and in India.

PLATE 325. *Drawing by Wilhelm Nicolai Marstrand, 1840.* $7 \times 4\frac{1}{4}$ in. No. 3055.

PHILIP WILLIAM MAY. 1864–1903.

A caricaturist, poster artist and cartoonist who was born in Leeds, spent three years in Australia where he worked on the *Sydney Bulletin*, but is best-known for his contributions to *Punch* and *The Graphic*, generally illustrating London scenes and characters—East End and West End.

PLATE 326. *Drawing by himself.* $5\frac{1}{2} \times 4\frac{1}{4}$ in. No. 3038.

SIR HENRY IRVING. 1838–1905.

He established his reputation as a tragedian of power and originality with his *Hamlet* at the Lyceum (1874–5) and for twenty-one years, in memorable partnership with Ellen Terry, he remained at the head of the profession. He was the first actor to be knighted (1895).

PLATE 327. *Painting by Jules Bastien Lepage, 1880.* 17×18 in. No. 1560.

ELLEN (NELLIE) FARREN. 1848–1904.

Born in a distinguished theatrical family, she was a favourite at the Gaiety Theatre (1868–91) where she played in everything from farce, burlesque and comic opera to Restoration comedy and Shakespeare, specialising in boys' parts. 'Miss Farren', said a contemporary critic, 'may be a wife and a mother, but she is certainly one of the best boys in existence.'

PLATE 328. *Painting by Walford Graham Robertson, 1902.* $30\frac{1}{2} \times 24$ in. No. 3133.

DAME ELLEN ALICE TERRY. 1847–1928.

The most accomplished member of a family of actors. Her stage career started when she was a child, and she made her last appearance at the age of seventy-eight, but her greatest triumphs belong to the years of her association with Sir Henry Irving between 1878 and 1902. Her charm and beauty, her thrilling voice, her gaiety and bubbling enthusiasm, together with her very great mastery of technique, made her the most entrancing personality in the history of the English stage.

PLATE 329. *Painting by Sir Johnston Forbes-Robertson, 1876.* $23\frac{1}{2} \times 19\frac{1}{2}$ in. No. 3789.

DINAH MARIA MULOCK (Mrs Craik). 1826–1887.
She was possibly the only Victorian woman novelist to approach the rarefied atmosphere inhabited by George Eliot, her sole outstanding work being *John Halifax, Gentleman* (1857), which illustrates the doctrine that the character of a gentleman resides in integrity of purpose rather than in birth and wealth.

PLATE 330. *Painting by Sir Hubert von Herkomer, 1887.* 47½ × 36½ in. No. 3304.

OCTAVIA HILL. 1838–1912.
A social reformer who, deeply shocked in her youth by the London slums, devoted her many abilities to housing reform, open space preservation and smoke abatement. She also helped to found the National Trust.

PLATE 331. *Painting by John Singer Sargent, 1899.* 39¾ × 30½ in. No. 1746.

JOSEPHINE ELIZABETH BUTLER (née Grey). 1828–1906.
A social reformer, particularly remembered for her work on contagious diseases and the white slave traffic, her crusades extending to Europe and India. She enlisted the help of Florence Nightingale, Harriet Martineau and, in Parliament, Sir James Stanfeld.

PLATE 332. *Painting by George Frederic Watts.* 29½ × 24½ in. No. 2194.

HORATIO HERBERT KITCHENER, 1st EARL KITCHENER. 1850–1916.
He made his name by organising the Egyptian army, crushing the Sudanese dervishes at Omdurman (1898) and planning the new city of Khartoum. In the South African War he succeeded Lord Roberts as Commander-in-Chief (1900). In 1914, as Secretary-of-State for War, he virtually created a new army and in less than eighteen months placed seventy divisions in the field. He was drowned in H.M.S. *Hampshire* on the way to advise the Tsar on reorganising the Russian armies.

PLATE 333. *Painting by Sir Hubert von Herkomer, 1890.* 55 × 43 in. No. 1782.

FREDERICK SLEIGH ROBERTS, 1st EARL ROBERTS. 1832–1914.
His career as a soldier ranges from the Indian Mutiny when he won the

V.C. (1858), to the outbreak of war in 1914 when he died in Flanders as Colonel-in-Chief of United Kingdom forces. He distinguished himself in the Afghan wars, as Commander-in-Chief both in India and South Africa, and in the years before the first world war, by leading a campaign at home for national military service.

PLATE 334. *Painting by George Frederic Watts, 1898.* $29\frac{1}{4} \times 24\frac{1}{4}$ in. No. 1744.

JOSEPH CHAMBERLAIN. 1836–1914.

Retiring early from a successful business career he was drawn into politics by his interest in social reforms, and though his proposals were not in themselves so very revolutionary, his energy—even violence— in presenting them upset many people. His unshakable belief in the paramount importance of imperial unity led to a split with Gladstone over Irish home rule. Later as Colonial Secretary under Lord Salisbury he used every means to strengthen the bonds with the self governing colonies and to develop, and foster trade with, the Crown colonies. He strove by means of conciliation and negotiation to prevent the South African War: when it was over, his wisdom and moderation in dealing with racial and political differences surely laid the foundations for the ultimate Union of South Africa.

PLATE 335. *Painting by Frank Holl, 1886.* $45\frac{1}{2} \times 34$ in. No. 1604.

JOHN BURNS. 1858–1943.

He was a formidable socialist agitator in the 1880's, but joined Campbell-Bannerman's administration of 1905 and became the first 'working man' to rise to the rank of Cabinet Minister.

PLATE 336. *Painting by The Hon. John Collier, 1889.* $49 \times 36\frac{1}{4}$ in. No. 3170.

KING EDWARD VII. 1841–1910.

Eldest son of Queen Victoria. He travelled extensively and acquired a deep understanding of human nature and of international diplomacy. During his mother's long life he was jealously excluded from official responsibility in public affairs, but his innate gifts, his genial charm, tact and persuasiveness, his wide acquaintance with foreign personalities, and his 'unique power of combining bonhomie with dignity' enabled him to exert an important influence in the cause of peace. By the time he eventually came to the throne in 1901 he enjoyed world-wide and unrivalled popularity.

PLATE 337. *Painting by Sir Luke Fildes.* $108\frac{1}{2} \times 71$ in. No. 1691.

ALEXANDRA OF DENMARK. 1844–1925.

Daughter of Christian IX, King of Denmark, she married the Prince of Wales, later King Edward VII, in 1863, and became first a leader of fashion, then a great and beloved Queen, and finally a worker for the relief of suffering, giving her name to 'Alexandra Day' and 'Queen Alexandra's Nurses'.

PLATE 338. *Painting by Sir Luke Fildes.* 50½ × 40½ in. No. 1889.

GEORGE NATHANIEL CURZON, 1ST MARQUESS CURZON. 1859–1925.

After an early career of great promise he became Viceroy of India in 1898, a position, suited to his naturally autocratic habits and impelling imperialism, wherein he performed prodigious feats of industry and achieved unprecedented heights of magnificence. Some unfortunate differences led up to his resignation in 1905, and for eleven years he was concerned mainly with the fine arts and the preservation of ancient monuments, and with university reform. From 1919 he was Foreign Secretary, and his spectacular domination of the Lausanne conference was his great diplomatic triumph. Ill health made him intractable and difficult to work with; his manner, likened to that of 'a divinity addressing black beetles', was not endearing and a lack of flexibility prevented his brilliant gifts from being used to the greatest advantage.

PLATE 339. *Painting by J. Cooke after J. S. Sargent.* 41 × 32 in. No. 2534.

ROBERT FALCON SCOTT. 1868–1912.

Naval captain and commander of two expeditions to the Antarctic. On his second expedition he and four companions, Wilson, Oates, Bowers and Evans, reached the South Pole a few weeks after Amundsen, and perished on the return journey, storm-bound a few miles from provisions. His journal, in which he made the last entry when dying, is in the British Museum.

PLATE 340. *Painting by Daniel Albert Wehrschmidt, 1905.* 59½ × 39½ in. No. 2079.

SIR JOHN WILLIAM ALCOCK. 1892–1919.

In June 1919, with Arthur Whitten Brown as navigator, he made the first flight across the Atlantic, from St John's, Newfoundland, to Clifden, Ireland. Six months later he was killed in a flying accident near Rouen.

PLATE 341. *Painting by Ambrose McEvoy, 1919.* 59 × 40 in. No. 1894.

DOUGLAS HAIG, 1st EARL HAIG. 1861–1928.

Field-Marshal. He fought with distinction in the Sudan and South Africa, and in 1909 was appointed Chief-of-Staff in India. In 1914 he took the First Army Corps to France, and from 1915 till the end of the war was Commander-in-Chief of the British Forces in France and Flanders. Thereafter he worked untiringly for the welfare of ex-service men: the British Legion and the United Services Fund were both the result of his endeavours.

PLATE 342. *From a group by John Singer Sargent.* No. 1954.

DAVID BEATTY, 1st EARL BEATTY. 1871–1936.

Admiral. The youngest Flag Officer since Nelson, he became Naval Secretary to Churchill. He commanded the battle cruiser squadron at Heligoland in 1914 and at the battle of Jutland in 1916, and was Commander of the Grand Fleet 1916-18.

PLATE 343. *From a group by Sir Arthur Stockdale Cope.* No. 1913.

JOHN DENTON PINKSTONE FRENCH, 1st EARL OF YPRES. 1852–1925.

Field-Marshal. In 1914 he was Commander-in-Chief of the British Expeditionary Force in France and Flanders, but during the first difficult and confused months of the war he was unable to achieve any decisive results and at the end of 1915 he resigned and was succeeded by Haig. In the newly created post of Commander-in-Chief of the Home Forces he reorganised military training and home defence: he also had to deal with the troubles in Ireland. He was Lord Lieutenant from 1919 till 1921 when the Government of Ireland bill was passed.

PLATE 344. *Painting by John Singer Sargent.* $21\frac{1}{2} \times 15\frac{1}{2}$ in. No. 2654.

EDMUND HENRY HYNMAN ALLENBY, 1st VISCOUNT ALLENBY. 1861–1936.

Field-Marshal. He served under French and Haig on the western front from 1914 till 1917 when he took command of the British Expeditionary Force based on Egypt and conducted a masterly campaign against the Turks in Palestine. In 1919 he was appointed High Commissioner for Egypt and in 1922 secured the recognition of that country as a sovereign state.

PLATE 345. *Pastel by Eric Henri Kennington.* $17\frac{1}{2} \times 13\frac{1}{4}$ in. No. 2906.

COVENTRY KERSEY DIGHTON PATMORE. 1823–1896.

After twenty years in the Department of Printed Books at the British Museum, he turned to writing poetry, his theme, in such works as *The*

Angel in the House, being the conviction that human love is the reflection of divine love. His work on metrical structure is valued by prosodists.

PLATE 346. *Painting by John Singer Sargent, 1894.* 36 × 24 in. No. 1079.

SIR ARTHUR WING PINERO. 1855–1934.

A most accomplished and successful playwright who took a part with Wilde and, later, Shaw in reviving the English theatre. His fifty-four plays written in fifty-five years show great variety—from the early farces to the 'problem plays' such as *His House in Order*, *The Gay Lord Quex* or *The Second Mrs Tanqueray* in which Mrs Patrick Campbell first became famous—but all show his outstanding technical skill and craftsmanship.

PLATE 347. *Painting by Joseph Mordecai, 1891.* 49½ × 39½ in. No. 2761.

HENRY JAMES. 1843–1916.

American-born writer who felt himself irresistibly attracted to European life and culture and who settled in England in 1876, eventually becoming naturalised. He was a minute observer of human beings within the limited sphere of his experience, and his novels give meticulous analyses of states of mind; in many of them the mainspring of the action, if such it can be called, is in the contrast between the habits of thought in the Old World and in the New. He affected a ponderously convoluted manner of writing, and, indeed, of talking—'a sort of Chinese nest of parentheses'. Besides some twenty novels, which include *The American, Daisy Miller, What Maisie Knew, The Ambassadors* and *The Golden Bowl*, he wrote a great many stories and, to his chagrin less successfully, several plays.

PLATE 348. *Painting by John Singer Sargent, 1913.* 33½ × 26 in. No. 1767.

WILLIAM WYMARK JACOBS. 1863–1943.

Born at Wapping, the son of a wharf manager, he was a civil servant until the success of his early books allowed him to retire in 1898 and devote himself to writing. His works are mostly humorous nautical and longshore yarns, such as *Many Cargoes*, with some notable and macabre exceptions such as *The Monkey's Paw* which has been successful as a play and as a film.

PLATE 349. *Painting by Carton Moore-Park, 1910.* 26½ × 21 in. No. 3178.

THE SELECTING JURY OF THE NEW ENGLISH ART CLUB.

The New English Art Club is an exhibiting society which was started in 1885 to counter Academic rejection of new idioms in art. Among the early members or exhibitors were Whistler, Sargent, Brabazon, Sickert, Steer, Tonks, Fry, Conder, McEvoy, Orpen and John.

PLATE 350. *Painting by Sir William Orpen, 1909.* 27½ × 35½ in. No. 2556. *The members shown are Dugald Sutherland MacColl, Alfred William Rich, Frederick Brown, Arthur Ambrose McEvoy, Sir William Rothenstein, Sir William Orpen, Walter Richard Sickert, Philip Wilson Steer, Augustus Edwin John and Henry Tonks.*

WALTER RICHARD SICKERT. 1860–1942.

Painter, lithographer and wit. At first a disciple of Whistler, in his *genre* pieces and townscapes he formed a style of his own which, in colour and tonality, is highly individual. His Venetian and Dieppe pieces are especially characteristic, as are his 'Camden Town' interiors and music-hall scenes.

PLATE 351. *Painting by Philip Wilson Steer.* 23½ × 11¾ in. No. 3142.

PHILIP WILSON STEER. 1860–1942.

The greatest English landscape painter since Turner. He fused his early schooling in French Impressionism with the influence that Constable and Turner had on him. His art is a synthesis of those two masters, developed into a wholly personal vision and expression.

PLATE 352. *Painting by Walter Richard Sickert.* 35½ × 23½ in. No. 3116.

KING GEORGE V. 1865–1936.

The younger son of Edward VII whom he succeeded in 1910. He was trained for the Navy and travelled widely in early life. By his wise handling of the many crises that he was called upon to meet during the twenty-six years of his reign he, no less than his father and grandmother, enhanced the prestige of the crown.

PLATE 353. *'The Royal Family at Buckingham Palace'. Painting by Sir John Lavery, 1913.* 134 × 107 in. No. 1745.

MARY OF TECK. 1867–1953.

The daughter of Francis, Duke of Teck and great-granddaughter of George III. She married the Duke of York, later King George V in 1893. She took little part in political affairs but was devoted to her family, and keenly interested in art and antiquities and in the care of the royal collections. The unflinching devotion, dignity and charm with which she carried out her onerous duties won the very deep affection of the nation.

PLATE 353. *'The Royal Family at Buckingham Palace' by Sir John Lavery, 1913.* 134 × 107 in. No. 1745.

GILBERT KEITH CHESTERTON. 1874–1936.

Though it amused him to call himself a journalist, he was distinguished in all branches of the art of literature. His weapons in defence of the traditional and religious elements of society were jest and paradox, but the serious sincerity of his philosophy was not obscured by his superb foolery. Some of his most popular works were *The Napoleon of Notting Hill, The Man who was Thursday* and the 'Father Brown' stories; perhaps of greater moment were *Orthodoxy, The Everlasting Man* and the studies of Browning, Dickens and Stevenson: his verse included *The Ballad of the White Horse* and a very nice line in 'hate poems'.

PLATE 354. *Painting by Herbert James Gunn, 1932.* 59½ × 43½ in. No. 3654.

THE HON. MAURICE BARING. 1874–1945.

Man of letters. His deep grounding in the classics and familiarity with European literature, particularly Russian, and the experience of his early years in the diplomatic corps, give a great breadth and mellowness to his work. His most memorable books are *Unreliable History* (1935) and the anthology *Have You Anything to Declare?* (1936).

PLATE 354. *Painting by Herbert James Gunn, 1932.* 59½ × 43½ in. No. 3654.

JOSEPH HILAIRE PIERRE BELLOC. 1870–1953.

He was two years old when his French father died and he was brought home by his English mother to be brought up and educated in this country: at the age of thirty he was naturalised. He and Chesterton became extremely lively companions in arms in defence of liberalism and the age-long wisdom of mankind against the forces of heresy and revolution. His energy and rollicking zest produced a spate of essays, novels, verse, travel books, biography and criticism. Among his best-known works are *The Path to Rome* and *The Four Men* which tells of Sussex, the shire he made peculiarly his own.

PLATE 354. *Painting by Herbert James Gunn, 1932.* 59½ × 43½ in. No. 3654.

RUPERT BROOKE. 1887–1915.

His lyrics, the nostalgic *Old Vicarage, Grantchester* and the 1914 group of sonnets showed the presence of genius and gave promise of greater things. His goodwill, good looks and charm made him greatly loved: Henry James called him 'a creature on whom the gods had smiled their brightest'—and he died young, of blood poisoning contracted at Scyros whither his war service in the Royal Naval Division had carried him.

PLATE 355. *Drawing by James Havard Thomas, posthumous.* 16¾ in. diameter. No. 2448.

GEORGE BERNARD SHAW. 1856–1950.

Early in life he left his native Ireland for London, practised as music, art and literary critic, and became a leader of the Fabian socialists, outstanding as orator and pamphleteer. His iconoclasm and delight in mocking, shocking, scandalising and ridiculing, together with the power of a born humorist to evoke gusty laughter, earned for his plays a sensational and noisy success which enabled him to use the theatre as a pulpit wherefrom to preach the social philosophy which he expounded at length in the Prefaces to his plays, in *The Intelligent Woman's Guide to Socialism and Capitalism* and in *The Adventures of a Black Girl in her Search for God.* He wrote fifty or more plays, the last of them when he was enjoying the role of internationally famous nonagenarian.

PLATE 356. *Caricature by Harry Furniss.* 6¼ × 3½ in. No. 3604.

ALFRED EDWARD HOUSMAN. 1859–1936.

One of our most distinguished classical scholars. The pessimistic impulse of his age found expression in *A Shropshire Lad* (1896) and *Last Poems* (1922), verses of an exquisite classical cast which had a wide influence among the 'Georgian' school of poets.

PLATE 357. *Drawing by Francis Dodd, 1926.* 14¾ × 10¾ in. No. 3075.

JOSEPH CONRAD. 1857–1924.

A naturalised Englishman of Polish birth and parentage, he served in the French, and then in the British merchant marine until, in 1894, he gave up seafaring for writing. Almost immediately his books won a *succès d'estime*, but it was not till 1914 that he suddenly achieved wide popularity. Many of his stories describe his own experiences during his life at sea; his natural gift for story telling and the perfect command of English which he acquired enabled him to communicate with unusual vividness the peculiar intensity of his emotion and perception. Among his many famous novels are *The Nigger of the Narcissus, Lord Jim, Nostromo, Chance* and *The Rover.*

PLATE 358. *Etching by Walter Ernest Tittle, 1924.* $7\frac{1}{4} \times 6$ in. No. 2482.

ENOCH ARNOLD BENNETT. 1867–1931.

A versatile and extremely successful writer whose fame as a novelist rests on a type of realistic social study, set in the district of his birth—the five towns of the Staffordshire potteries—and presenting an uncompromisingly literal picture of lower middle-class life in the industrial provinces. Among his most memorable works are *Anna of the Five Towns, The Old Wives' Tale,* the *Clayhanger* trilogy and, in a lighter mood, *The Grand Babylon Hotel* and *The Card.*

PLATE 359. *Drawing by Walter Ernest Tittle, 1923.* $10\frac{1}{2} \times 8$ in. No. 2664.

SIR JAMES MATTHEW BARRIE, BART. 1860–1937.

Scottish writer who moved to London at the age of twenty-five and enjoyed a long and distinguished literary career. His first successful books, *A Widow in Thrums* and *The Little Minister,* were followed by a number of gently satirical plays such as *The Professor's Love Story, Quality Street* and *The Admirable Crichton.* Later productions which, despite a touch of whimsy and occasional mawkishness, were also very successful included *A Kiss for Cinderella, Dear Brutus* and *Mary Rose.* Best known of all his plays, first produced in 1904 and revived annually, is the sentimental fantasy for children, *Peter Pan.*

PLATE 360. *Drawing by Walter Thomas Monnington, 1932.* $12\frac{3}{4} \times 9$ in. No. 3539.

THOMAS EDWARD LAWRENCE. 1888–1935.

'Lawrence of Arabia.' As an archaeologist working at Carchemish, and in lonely wanderings, he acquired a knowledge of the Arabs and their language. During the war of 1914-18 he showed himself a leader of genius, with extraordinary enterprise, courage and military skill, when he rallied the Arab tribes in revolt against Turkey, won their allegiance and, living as one of themselves, using always 'the smallest force, in the quickest time, at the furthest place', won repeated successes and distracted large enemy forces, so giving invaluable help to Allenby's army. Having done his best in the Arab interest at the Peace Conference and when in the Colonial Office in 1921-2, he retired and joined the R.A.F. as a private. Thereafter he clung to obscurity, changing his name more than once; a motor-bicycle accident led to his untimely death. *The Seven Pillars of Wisdom* is his account of the Arab revolt, *The Mint* a description of life in the Air Force.

PLATE 361. *Drawing by Augustus Edwin John.* 14 × 10 in. No. 3187.

DAVID LLOYD GEORGE, 1ST EARL LLOYD GEORGE. 1863–1945.

He first entered the political field as a Welsh Nationalist, but was soon recognised as one of the leaders of the Liberal party, and was Chancellor of the Exchequer from 1908 till 1915, during which time he introduced his National Insurance schemes. In 1915 he became Minister of Munitions and the following year succeeded Mr Asquith as Prime Minister. His personal magnetism and flamboyant opportunism made him a popular war-time leader, but his prestige began perceptibly to decline at the Versailles Peace Conference.

PLATE 362. *Painting by Sir William Orpen, 1927.* 37 × 35 in. No. 3244.

HERBERT HENRY ASQUITH, 1ST EARL OF OXFORD AND ASQUITH. 1852–1928.

He practised at the bar with notable success, but his interest was in politics and he soon came to the fore as a Liberal leader. In 1892 he became Home Secretary, in 1905 Chancellor of the Exchequer, and Prime Minister in 1908. During his eight years of office many badly needed reforms were instituted, the constitutional crisis of 1911 was weathered and the Irish Home Rule bill passed. He remained in office for the first two years of the first world war and was subjected to much ignorant criticism and unscrupulous attack; in 1916 he was succeeded by Lloyd George. He has been called 'the last of the Romans' and indeed his integrity and restraint and the calm deliberate periods of his fine oratory were in the great tradition of statesmanship.

PLATE 363. *Painting by André Cluysenaar, 1919.* 34 × 24½ in. No. 2361.

EDWARD GREY, 1ST VISCOUNT GREY. 1862–1933.

As Foreign Secretary from 1905 to 1916 he did much to keep the peace during the difficult years before 1914, and much also to strengthen the ties of common interest and friendship binding England to France, Russia and America; thus, though in the end he was powerless to avert the war, it was largely thanks to his policy that Germany was defeated. His book, *Twenty-five Years*, is an account of his public career. In private life—perhaps of more importance to him—he was a great naturalist, fisherman and bird-lover, as can be seen from his books *Fallodon Papers* and *The Charm of Birds*.

PLATE 364. *Painting by Sir James Guthrie.* $33\frac{1}{2} \times 28\frac{1}{2}$ in. No. 3545.

RICHARD BURDON HALDANE, 1ST VISCOUNT HALDANE. 1856–1928.

Lawyer, philosopher and statesman. As Secretary of State for War from 1905 to 1912 he carried out drastic and vital army reforms, creating the Territorial Army and Expeditionary Force on which so much depended in 1914. He was twice Lord Chancellor, and he also did a very great deal for the furtherance of higher education and the improvement of public administration.

PLATE 365. *Painting by Philip Alexius László de Lombos, 1928.* $38\frac{1}{4} \times 28\frac{3}{4}$ in. No. 2364.

JAMES RAMSAY MACDONALD. 1866–1937.

Of humble Scottish birth, and self educated. He joined the Fabian Society in 1886. Later he became a leader of the Labour party, and eventually the first Labour Prime Minister. His moderation was violently resented by extreme socialists during the unrestful years 1911–14 and during the war it made him widely and intensely unpopular: confidence in him revived as he successfully steered the Labour party away from revolutionary communism towards parliamentary socialism. The financial crisis of 1931 caused a split in his Labour cabinet, and from then until 1935, when he retired, he was at the head of the 'National', all-party government.

PLATE 366. *Bronze bust by Sir Jacob Epstein, 1934.* 24 in. high. No. 2934.

JOHN BUCHAN, 1ST BARON TWEEDSMUIR. 1875–1940.

His delight was in writing which he did continuously from before his undergraduate days to the end of his life, no matter what other work he was doing at the same time. He was made Governor-General of Canada in 1935, and his wise statesmanship, unsparing devotion, sympathy and charm won universal respect and affection. Besides the widely popular adventure stories such as *Prester John* and the trilogy, *The Thirty-nine Steps, Greenmantle* and *Mr Standfast*, he wrote a number of histories and biographies, for example, *Montrose, Oliver Cromwell* and *Augustus*.

PLATE 367. *Bronze bust by Thomas J. Clapperton, 1935.* 14 in. high. No. 3636.

STANLEY BALDWIN, 1ST EARL BALDWIN.
1867–1947.

He was three times Prime Minister between 1923 and 1937, the period being marked by such problems as the general strike in 1926 and the abdication of King Edward VIII. His attitude towards the menace of German and Italian totalitarianism was much criticised, especially after the outbreak of war.

PLATE 368. *Painting by Reginald Grenville Eves.* $30\frac{3}{4} \times 26$ in. No. 3551.

GEORGE LANSBURY. 1859–1940.

Labour leader and pacifist, widely known as 'The John Bull of Poplar', he is mainly identified with the bettering of conditions in the East End of London, the founding of the Labour newspaper, the *Daily Herald*, and the championship of conscientious objectors. While First Commissioner of Works in the second Labour government he created the so-called 'Lansbury Lido' in Hyde Park.

PLATE 369. *Painting by Sylvia Laura Gosse.* $20\frac{1}{2} \times 13\frac{1}{2}$ in. No. 3775.

SIR WILLIAM HENRY BRAGG. 1862–1942.

His most distinguished work was in the field of crystalline analysis and X-ray spectroscopy, in his advocacy of research in industry, and in popular exposition. He inaugurated the famous Christmas lectures to children at the Royal Institution.

PLATE 370. *Drawing by Randoph Schwabe, 1932.* $11\frac{1}{2} \times 8\frac{1}{8}$ in. No. 3255.

SIR JOSEPH JOHN THOMSON. 1856–1940.

The discovery of the electron, which he first made public in a Friday Evening Discourse at the Royal Institution on 30th April, 1897, is by general consent due to him, and it brought in its train the advances in physical science of the twentieth century.

PLATE 371. *Drawing by Walter Thomas Monnington, 1932.* $15\frac{1}{2} \times$ 12 in. No. 3256.

ERNEST RUTHERFORD, 1st BARON RUTHERFORD. 1871–1937.

Born in New Zealand, he came to England in 1894 to work at Cambridge under J. J. Thomson. His discoveries were pioneering in the field of radio-activity. He was the first to recognise the nuclear nature of the atom. He was ideally equipped to direct a physical laboratory and could kindle an enthusiasm that amounted almost to devotion.

PLATE 372. *Painting by Herbert James Gunn, 1932.* 30 × 25 in. No. 2935.

SIR RONALD ROSS. 1857–1932.

For a time a ship's surgeon, later in the Indian Medical Service, he eventually specialised in tropical medicine and bacteriology. Working with Sir Patrick Manson he discovered in 1898 the function of the mosquito in the malaria cycle, thus showing where to direct the attack in attempting to bring that most deadly of tropical diseases under control. He was a man of wide and varied interests, a considerable mathematician and the author of poems, dramas and novels.

PLATE 373. *Bronze relief by Frank Bowcher, 1929.* $6\frac{3}{4} \times 5\frac{3}{4}$ in. No. 3646.

BEATRIX POTTER (MRS W. HEELIS). Died 1943.

She wrote and illustrated stories about small familiar animals for small children, and successive generations have delighted in her practical fantasies and have been close friends of Peter Rabbit, Benjamin Bunny, Mrs Tabitha Twitchit, Mrs Tiggy-Winkle and many other unforgettable characters. She was a breeder of sheep on her Cumberland farm.

PLATE 374. *Painting by Delmar Harmood Banner, 1938.* 30 × 25 in. No. 3635.

DAME ETHEL MARY SMYTH. 1858–1944.

She studied music in Leipzig for seven years, and a number of her compositions were first performed in Germany. In defence of the rights of women, both in politics and, more particularly, as creative artists entitled to serious attention, she fought valiantly, ferociously and persistently—and victoriously in that she was the first woman to have a major work, the Mass in D, performed at the Albert Hall and an opera, *The Wreckers* for one, at Covent Garden. Her musical output was large and she wrote besides a number of volumes of vivid autobiography.

PLATE 375. *Drawing by John Singer Sargent.* $23\frac{1}{2} \times 18\frac{1}{2}$ in. No. 3243.

EMMELINE PANKHURST (NÉE GOULDEN). 1858–1928.

Leader of the 'Votes for Women' movement. Moderate agitation meeting with indifferent success, from 1905 till 1914 she and her rapidly growing army of suffragettes adopted increasingly violent, sensational and lawless methods. On the outbreak of war she called a truce to militancy; it was largely the part played by women during the next four years that compelled recognition of their claim to equal rights with men, and an act passed in 1918 was a step towards the Representation of the People Act of 1928, which gave full and equal suffrage to men and women.

PLATE 376. *Painting by Georgina Brackenbury, 1927.* 31 × 24½ in. No. 2360.

SIR EDWARD WILLIAM ELGAR, BART. 1857–1934.

From youth he was associated with music-making in Worcestershire, and in early manhood gave up his intention of becoming a concert violinist to concentrate on composing. After the *Enigma Variations*, first performed in 1899 under Richter, his was recognised as the leading name in English music. Other well-known works which also show his remarkable gift for orchestration are the oratorio *The Dream of Gerontius*, the symphonic study *Falstaff*, and the Violin Concerto, which was first played by Kreisler in 1910. The tune known as 'Land of Hope and Glory' which comes in the first of his *Pomp and Circumstance* marches is almost as familiar as the national anthem.

PLATE 377. *Bronze bust by Percival M. E. Hedley, 1927.* 18½ in. high. No. 2219.

SIR HENRY JOSEPH WOOD. 1869–1944.

His enthusiasm, energy and single-minded devotion made him the most widely popular musical figure of his, and probably any other, time. Not only did he teach and encourage young musicians, form choirs and orchestras, organise and conduct concerts; it may be said that, by instilling an appreciation of music in a vast middle-brow section of the British public, he created also a permanent concert audience. This feat was achieved largely by means of the Promenade Concerts which he conducted for fifty consecutive seasons and which are still known by his name.

PLATE 378. *Painting by Frank O. Salisbury, 1943.* 43 × 32½ in. No. 3688.

ADELINE VIRGINIA WOOLF (née Stephen).
1882–1941.
A daughter of Sir Leslie Stephen, she became the leading lady of the Bloomsbury group of writers in the 1920's. Her own work, in criticism, in essays, but most remarkably in her novels, such as *The Waves*, shows a new and decisive perception of the shifting indecision of all things in time.
PLATE 379. *Lead bust by The Hon. Stephen Tomlin.* 16 in. high. No. 3882.

WILLIAM BUTLER YEATS. 1865–1939.
Irish poet, playwright and visionary; at one time the leader of the 'Celtic Twilight' school. The performance (thanks largely to Lady Gregory) of his verse play, *The Countess Cathleen*, in Dublin in 1899 marks the foundation of the Irish theatre. As director of the Abbey Theatre he gave energetic support to J. M. Synge and other younger writers. In 1922 he became a member of the Irish Senate.
PLATE 380. *Bronze bust by Kathleen Scott, 1907.* 18 in. high. No. 3644 A.

JAMES AUGUSTINE ALOYSIUS JOYCE. 1882–1941.
Born in Dublin, he spent most of his adult life on the Continent. The publication of his novel *Ulysses* caused some commotion, and a number of writers imitated his manner, especially his use of the 'interior monologue'. Although some critics maintained that his anarchic disintegration of the English language and his 'word-coinage' were carried so far as to make him incomprehensible, the censorious found his obscenity clear enough, and *Ulysses* was banned in England and America. Among his works are *A Portrait of the Artist as a Young Man*, *Finnegans Wake* and two small volumes of verse.
PLATE 381. *Painting by Jacques Emile Blanche, 1935.* $49\frac{1}{4} \times 34\frac{1}{4}$ in. No. 3883.

KING GEORGE VI. 1895–1952.
He served in the Royal Navy and fought at the battle of Jutland in 1916, and also in the Royal Air Force. While Duke of York he founded the camps for public-school and working-class boys which he frequently attended himself and to which he gave his name, and he was actively interested in questions of industrial welfare. He came to the throne on

the abdication of his elder brother in 1936 and quickly won the very deep respect and affection of his subjects in England and throughout the Commonwealth. His wisdom and sympathy, and his resolute and steadfast bearing through all the bitterness of the second world war were an inspiration and a comfort to the nation.

PLATE 382. *'Conversation Piece at the Royal Lodge, Windsor'* by Herbert James Gunn, 1950. $59\frac{1}{2} \times 39\frac{1}{2}$ in. No. 3778.

INDEX OF SITTERS

INDEX OF ARTISTS

264

265